D1234577

THE GEORGICS OF VIRGIL

THE
GEORGICS
OF VIRGIL

TRANSLATED BY C. DAY LEWIS

WITH AN INTRODUCTION BY LOUIS BROMFIELD

NEW YORK · OXFORD UNIVERSITY PRESS · 1947

          . . . there's so much war in the world,
Evil has so many faces, the plough so little
Honour, the labourers are taken, the fields untended,
And the curving sickle is beaten into the sword that yields not.

There the East is in arms, here Germany marches:
Neighbour cities, breaking their treaties, attack each other:
The wicked War-god runs amok through all the world.

Georgics, Book I, 11. 505-11

INTRODUCTION

By Louis Bromfield

IT IS remarkable how many of the writers and particularly the poets of the world have been closely associated with the land and the delights of rural life. The variety runs all the way from the Greek Hesiod and the authors of some of the most beautiful passages of the Old Testament through Virgil and Voltaire and Jefferson into our time. It is a popular but fallacious belief that Voltaire was a sophisticated dweller in cities. Sophisticated in his times he certainly was, but it was not the shallow sophistication which marks too often the tactics, the fancies, and philosophy of the city dweller. It was a deeper, more eternal, more rugged knowledge and experience drawn out of Nature itself which endowed him with a ferocious and belligerent sense of liberty and justice. Even Pope, one of the most artificial and sometimes brittle poets, chose a country life throughout most of his existence.

But no poet has told more beautifully or richly the delights and satisfactions of country existence than the great Virgil, nor has any poet related those pleasures in terms more eternal and universal. Virgil did not write of the delights of a rural existence in the flowery romantic fashion of Rousseau or in the colors of Fragonard and Boucher. He wrote of the farm, of garden and vineyard, of cattle and horsebreeding, of manuring the fields, with all the knowledge and instinct of a practising and a practical farmer, always in a strong verse which at times in its feeling becomes heroic. At times the Gods and Goddesses descend into his fields, and history, legend, and even allegory play their roles. There is in *The Georgics* that deep sense of religion and faith which is in every good farmer.

It is quite evident that Virgil was a good husbandman and that no neighbor could sell him a spavined horse or a poor unprofitable cow. He knew what makes fertile soil and understood the vagaries of weather and how to deal with them. He enjoyed the rural market place and the feel of good fleece and the points which made a good cow both for producing milk and for drawing the plow.

The Georgics are a treatise upon the agriculture and livestock breeding of Virgil's time, told in high poetry with all the dignity of the good husbandman which one senses in such a man wherever one finds him in the world. He knew the feel of good soil beneath his feet and the signs auguring a cold blast from the Alps. He could not sleep if his cattle were hungry or ill-sheltered.

A reading of *The Georgics* is fascinating not alone to the poet and philosopher of our day but to the farmer as well for in its pages one discovers how eternal is agriculture and how ancient is much of the knowledge practiced in the farming of today. In *The Georgics* are recorded many practices regarded until lately as superstitions for which science has found since a solid and real base in reason and fact.

Perhaps the most satisfactory quality of the whole poem is the fashion in which it creates for us the reality of Virgil's agricultural existence and activities. Turning the pages I can see his farm and his animals and his people and even his own stern and rugged figure moving across the landscape among the vineyards and flocks, visiting the barns and stables, watching his fields for signs of thinness in the soil and sickliness in plants.

The Georgics form a great and eternal poem for every kind of reader. I cannot help but believe that the good farmer who loves his fields and woods and streams will appreciate it most of all, for in Virgil he has met a man who might have sat beneath a tree or stood in a fence corner all day discussing with delight and unending enthusiasm the whole business of soil and markets, cattle and horses, and all those close bonds with nature which determine the character; the philosophy, and the spirit of every good farmer, whether he lives in Italy or China, in Nebraska or in Bengal.

LOUIS BROMFIELD

Malabar Farm
January 1947

FOREWORD

THE fascination of the Georgics for many generations of the English-speaking peoples is not difficult to explain. A century of urban civilization has not yet materially modified the instinct we inherit from ancestors devoted to agriculture and stock-breeding, to the chase, to landscape gardening, to a practical love of Nature. No poem yet written has touched these subjects with more expert knowledge or more tenderness than the Georgics. In our love of domestic animals, in the simple urge the town-dweller feels to get out into the country, we may see the depth and tenacity of our roots in earth to-day. It may, indeed, happen that the recent war, together with the spread of electrical power, will result in a decentralization of industry and the establishment of a new rural-urban civilization working through smaller social units. The factory in the fields need not remain a dream of poets and planners: it has more to commend it than the window-box in the slums.

For the translator, too, the Georgics have a special fascination. They are a work which is at once serious and charming, didactic and passionate; and didactic verse is the only kind which can be translated literally without losing the poetic quality of the original. The present translation is line for line, and literal except where a heightening of intensity in the original seemed to justify a certain freedom of interpretation.

I believe that every classical poem worth translating should be translated afresh every fifty years. The contemporary poetic idiom, whether it be derived chiefly from common speech or a literary tradition, will have changed sufficiently within that period to demand a new interpretation. To John Martyn, the Cambridge botanist, writing in 1740, Dryden's version of the Georgics already seemed to show bad taste in many passages; while to us more recent translations may appear vulgar or insipid, particularly when they are written in that peculiar kind of latin-derived pidgin-english which infects the style of so many classical scholars.

The important thing is to steer between the twin vulgarities of flashy colloquialism and perfunctory grandiloquence. This I have tried to do. I have also tried to render my translation as explicit as possible, because I made it chiefly for readers who have no Latin and because classical allusions have ceased to be commonplaces for even the highly educated. I have avoided footnotes, and attempted wherever I could to make these allusions explicit in the text (e.g. by translating 'Pales' as 'goddess of sheepfolds'). I had thought, also, of modernizing the geographical terms: but many of the places mentioned by Virgil are only doubtfully identified; the reader can be little enlightened by naming the river Strymon the river Struma, and the piling of Ossa on Pelion seems preferable to the piling of Kissovo on Plesnid.

As to the metre used here, it should be said that neither the heroic couplet nor the English hexameter — the two metres most commonly used in translations of the Georgics — seemed to me adequate now for the rendering of the Latin hexameter. After much experiment, I decided to use a rhythm based on the hexameter, containing six beats in each line, but allowing much variation of pace and interspersed with occasional short lines of three stresses. This metre, I hoped, would be elastic enough to avoid the monotony of the English hexameter, and more consonant with the speech-rhythms of the present day.

I owe many thanks to the friends whose interest in this translation encouraged me to continue with it during a time not favourable for such work: and particularly to Dr. C. M. Bowra, Warden of Wadham College, Oxford, for reading the MS. and making a number of criticisms; whatever defects of taste and scholarship remain are due solely to my own perseverance in error.

C. D. L.

April 1946

DEDICATORY STANZAS

To Stephen Spender

Poets are not in much demand these days—
We're red, it seems, or cracked, or bribed, or hearty
And, if invited, apt to spoil the party
With the oblique reproach of emigrés:
We cut no ice, although we're fancy skaters:
Aiming at art, we only strike the arty.
Poetry now, the kinder tell us, caters
For an elite: still, it gives us the hump
To think that we're the unacknowledged rump
Of a long parliament of legislators.

Where are the war poets? the fools inquire.
We were the prophets of a changeable morning
Who hoped for much but saw the clouds forewarning:
We were at war, while they still played with fire
And rigged the market for the ruin of man:
Spain was a death to us, Munich a mourning.
No wonder then if, like the pelican,
We have turned inward for our iron ration,
Tapping the vein and sole reserve of passion,
Drawing from poetry's capital what we can.

Yes, we shall fight, but—let them not mistake it—
Not for the ones who grudged to peace their pence
And gave war a blank cheque in self-defence,
Nor those who take self-interest and fake it

Into a code of honour—the distorting
Mirror those magnates hold to experience.
It's for dear life alone we shall be fighting,
The poet's living-space, the love of men,
And poets must speak for common suffering men
While history in sheets of fire is writing.

Meanwhile, what touches the heart at all, engrosses.
Through the flushed springtime and the fading year
I lived on country matters. Now June was here
Again, and brought the smell of flowering grasses
To me and death to many overseas:
They lie in the flowering sunshine, flesh once dear
To some, now parchment for the heart's release.
Soon enough each is called into the quarrel.
Till then, taking a leaf from Virgil's laurel,
I sang in time of war the arts of peace.

Virgil—a tall man, dark and countrified
In looks, they say: retiring: no rhetorician:
Of humble birth: a Celt, whose first ambition
Was to be a philosopher: Dante's guide.
But chiefly dear for his gift to understand
Earth's intricate, ordered heart, and for a vision
That saw beyond an imperial day the hand
Of man no longer armed against his fellow
But all for vine and cattle, fruit and fallow,
Subduing with love's positive force the land.

Different from his our age and myths, our toil
The same. Our exile and extravagances,

xvi

Revolt, retreat, fine faiths, disordered fancies
Are but the poet's search for a right soil
Where words may settle, marry, and conceive an
Imagined truth, for a regimen that enhances
Their natural grace. Now, as to one whom even
Our age's drought and spate have not deterred
From cherishing, like a bud of flame, the word,
I dedicate this book to you, dear Stephen.

Now, when war's long midwinter seems to freeze us
And numb our living sources once for all,
That veteran of Virgil's I recall
Who made a kitchen-garden by the Galaesus
On derelict land, and got the first of spring
From airs and buds, the first fruits in the fall,
And lived at peace there, happy as a king.
Naming him for good luck, I see man's native
Stock is perennial, and our creative
Winged seed can strike a root in anything.

June 1940

xvii

BOOK ONE

BOOK ONE

What makes the cornfields happy, under what constellation
It's best to turn the soil, my friend, and train the vine
On the elm; the care of cattle, the management of flocks,
The knowledge you need for keeping frugal bees: — all this
I'll now begin to relate. You brightest luminaries
Of the world, who head the year's parade across heaven's face:
Wine-god and kindly Harvest-goddess, if by your gift
Earth has exchanged the acorn for the rich ear of corn
And learnt to lace spring water with her discovered wine:
You Fauns, the tutelary spirits of country folk —
Dance here, you Fauns and Dryads —
Your bounties I celebrate. And you, Neptune, who first bade
The neighing horse start up from earth at your trident's stroke:
And you, the Forester, for whom three hundred head
Of milk-white cattle browse on the fruited bushes of Cea:
And you, leaving your native woods and the lawns of Arcadia,
Pan, master of flocks, if you love your Maenalus,
Come to my call and bless me: Minerva, who first discovered
The olive: the Boy who taught us the use of the crook-toothed plough:
Silvanus, bearing a young cypress plucked up by the roots: —
All gods and goddesses
Who care for the land, who nourish new fruits of the earth we sow not,
And send to our sown fields the plentiful rain from heaven.
You too, whatever place in the courts of the Immortals
Is soon to hold you — whether an overseer of cities
And warden of earth you'll be, Caesar, so that the great world
Honour you as promoter of harvest and puissant lord

[Lines 1-27]

Of the seasons, garlanding your brow with your mother's myrtle:
Or whether you come as god of the boundless sea, and sailors
Worship your power alone, and the ends of the earth pay tribute,
And Tethys gives all her waves to get you for son-in-law:
Or whether you make a new sign in the Zodiac, where amid the
Slow months a gap is revealed between Virgo and Scorpio
(Already the burning Scorpion retracts his claws to leave you
More than your share of heaven): —
Become what you may — and Hell hopes not for you as king,
And never may so ghastly a ruling ambition grip you,
Though Greece admire the Elysian Plains, and Proserpine
Care not to follow her mother who calls her back to earth —
Grant a fair passage, be gracious to this my bold design,
Pity with me the country people who know not the way,
Advance, and even now grow used to our invocations.

    Early spring, when a cold moisture sweats from the hoar-head
Hills and the brittle clods are loosening under a west wind,
Is the time for the bull to grunt as he pulls the plough deep-driven
And the ploughshare to take a shine, scoured clean in the furrow.
That crop, which twice has felt the sun's heat and the frost twice,
Will answer at last the prayers of the never-satisfied
Farmer, and burst his barns with an overflowing harvest.
But plough not an unknown plain:
First you must learn the winds and changeable ways of its weather,
The land's peculiar cultivation and character,
The different crops that different parts of it yield or yield not.
A corn-crop here, grapes there will come to the happier issue:
On another soil it is fruit trees, and grass of its own sweet will
Grows green. Look you, how Tmolus gives us the saffron perfume,
India its ivory, the unmanly Sabaeans their incense,
The naked Chalybes iron, Pontus the rank castor,

And Elis prize-winning mares.
Nature imposed these laws, a covenant everlasting,
On different parts of the earth right from the earliest days when
Deucalion cast over a tenantless world the stones
From which arose mankind, that dour race. Now, to business:
As soon as the first months of the year begin, your strong bulls
Should turn the fertile loam and leave the clods lying
For the full suns of summer to bake into a fine dust:
But if the land's not heavy, you'll find it enough at the North Star's
Rising to ridge it out in shallow furrows: — the one
Lest weeds should check the corn's exuberance, the other
Lest lack of moisture turn your soil to a sandy desert.
See, too, that your arable lies fallow in due rotation,
And leave the idle field alone to recoup its strength:
Or else, changing the seasons, put down to yellow spelt
A field where before you raised the bean with its rattling pods
Or the small-seeded vetch
Or the brittle stalk and rustling haulm of the bitter lupin.
For a crop of flax burns up a field, and so does an oat-crop,
And poppies drenched in oblivion burn up its energy.
Still, by rotation of crops you lighten your labour, only
Scruple not to enrich the dried-up soil with dung
And scatter filthy ashes on fields that are exhausted.
So too are the fields rested by a rotation of crops,
And unploughed land in the meanwhile promises to repay you.
Often again it profits to burn the barren fields,
Firing their light stubble with crackling flame: uncertain
It is whether the earth conceives a mysterious strength
And sustenance thereby, or whether the fire burns out
Her bad humours and sweats away the unwanted moisture,
Or whether that heat opens more of the ducts and hidden

5   [Lines 59-89]

Pores by which her juices are conveyed to the fresh vegetation,
Or rather hardens and binds her gaping veins against
Fine rain and the consuming sun's fierce potency
And the piercing cold of the north wind.
Much does he help his fields, moreover, who breaks with a mattock
Their lumpish clods and hauls the osier-harrow; on him
The golden goddess of corn looks down from heaven approving.
He helps them too, who raises ridges along the plain
With a first ploughing, and then cross-ploughs it, constantly
Exercising the soil and mastery over his acres.
Wet midsummers and fair winters are what the farmer
Should ask for; in winter's powdery dust the spelt will flourish,
The field is in good heart: Mysia can boast no better;
Given such weather, even Gargarus is mazed by its own harvests.
No need to commend him who, after the sowing, closely
Follows it up by breaking the clammy loam of the field,
Then lets in runnels of water to irrigate the seed-land
So that, when it is fever-parched and the green blade's failing,
Look! — from the hilltop he coaxes the water out of its course,
And it slides over smooth pebbles whispering hoarsely and soothes
The parched fields with its purling.
Another, for fear the cornstalk should wilt under the ear's weight,
Grazes down the exuberant crop while yet its young green
Is barely showing above the furrows: another makes
A gravel sump to collect and drain the standing damp,
Especially if in the doubtful months the river has flooded
And covered the water-meadows with a wide film of mud
So that the moisture steams in a warm mist up from the bottoms.
Yet, though men and oxen have laboured hard on these lines
Keeping the soil turned, still can the naughty goose
And cranes from the river Strymon and endive's bitter root

Do damage, and shade can be harmful. For the Father of agriculture
Gave us a hard calling: he first decreed it an art
To work the fields, sent worries to sharpen our mortal wits
And would not allow his realm to grow listless from lethargy.
Before Jove's time no settlers brought the land under subjection;
Not lawful even to divide the plain with landmarks and boundaries:
All produce went to a common pool, and earth unprompted
Was free with all her fruits.

Jove put the wicked poison in the black serpent's tooth,
Jove told the wolf to ravin, the sea to be restive always,
He shook from the leaves their honey, he had all fire removed,
And stopped the wine that ran in rivers everywhere,
So thought and experiment might forge man's various crafts
Little by little, asking the furrow to yield the corn-blade,
Striking the hidden fire that lies in the veins of flint.
Then first did alder-trunks hollowed out take the water;
Then did the mariner group and name the stars — the Pleiads,
Hyads and the bright Bear:
Then was invented the snare for taking game, the tricky
Bird-lime, the casting of hounds about the broad wood-coverts.
One whips now the wide river with casting-net and searches
Deep pools, another trawls his dripping line in the sea.
Then came the rigid strength of steel and the shrill saw-blade
(For primitive man was wont to split his wood with wedges);
Then numerous arts arose. Yes, unremitting labour
And harsh necessity's hand will master anything.
The Corn-goddess taught men first to turn the earth with iron —
That was the time when acorns and arbute berries grew scarce
In the sacred wood, and Dodona refused them sustenance.
Soon, too, the growing of corn became more arduous: vile blight
Attacked the stalks, and the shockheaded thistle sabotaged fields:

[Lines 121-151]

Crops fail, a prickly forest
Comes pushing up — goose-grass, star-thistle, unfeeding darnel
And barren wild-oats tyrannize over the shining tillage.
Unless you make war on the weeds relentlessly with your mattock
And scare the birds away, and pare with a bill-hook the darkening
Overgrowth of the country, and the rain has come to your call,
Vainly alas you will eye another man's heaped-up harvest
And relieve your own hunger by shaking an oak in the woods.
    I'll tell you too the armoury of the tough countryman,
For without this the harvest would neither be sown nor successful:
The ploughshare first and heavy timbers of the curving plough,
The ponderous-moving waggons that belong to the Mother of harvest,
Threshers and harrows and the immoderate weight of the mattock;
Slight implements, too, of osier,
Arbutus hurdles, the Wine-god's mystical winnowing-fan.
Be provident, lay by a stock of them long beforehand
If you wish to remain worthy of the land and its heaven-sent honour.
Early in woods the elm, by main force mastered, is bent
Into a share-beam and takes the shape of the curving plough:
Then to its stock are fitted a pole eight feet in length
And two earth-boards, and the share-head is set in its double back:
Light lime has been cut already for a yoke, and lofty beech
To make the handle that guides the whole affair from behind,
And the wood is hung up in chimneys where smoke will season it.
    Many the ancient saws I can relate, as long as
You're no quitter and willing to learn your modest craft.
Most urgent it is that the threshing-floor with a roller be flattened,
Wrought by hand, and reinforced with binding chalk,
Or else the dust may crack it and weeds come up through the chinks,
And various kinds of vermin play there: often the wee mouse
Builds underground his grange

And home, or the sightless mole scoops out his catacombs:
The toad is found in cavities, and all the manifold pests
Earth breeds; the enormous heap of spelt is spoiled by the weevil
And the ant that insures against a destitute old age.
Observe again, when the walnut clothes herself in the woods
With richest bloom and bends to earth her scented branches —
If her fruit is plentiful, a plentiful corn-crop follows,
And great will be the threshing in a season of great heat;
But if she is more luxuriant in shadowing leaves, you'll thresh
The corn quite fruitlessly for the straw will be full of chaff.
Many sowers indeed I have seen who doped their seed,
Bathing it first in natron or olive oil's black lees,
So the deceptive pods of the pulse might grow a bigger
Fruit, that should soften quickly even over a small fire.
I've noticed seed long chosen and tested with utmost care
Fall off, if each year the largest
Be not hand-picked by human toil. For a law of nature
Makes all things go to the bad, lose ground and fall away;
Just as an oarsman, when he is sculling his skiff against
The current, needs but relax the drive of his arms a little
And the current will carry him headlong away downstream.

    It is our task, again, to observe the star of Arcturus,
The days of the Kid, and the shining Serpent, as carefully
As sailors who homeward bound on windy waters are daring
The Black Sea and the straits by the oyster-beds of Abydos.
When the Scales make the hours for daytime and sleeptime balance,
Dividing the globe into equal hemispheres — light and darkness,
Then set your bulls to work, farmers, and sow your barley
Up to the last showers on the frost-bound limits of winter:
The flax-plant and corn-poppy
You should cover now in earth, and keep on hard at the ploughing

While a bone-dry soil allows it and the weather has not yet broken.
In spring you sow your beans: then too the softening furrows
Will take lucerne, and millet requires its annual care;
When the milk-white Bull with gilded horn begins the year
And the Dog Star drops away.
But if for a wheat harvest or crop of hardy spelt
You work your land, and are keen on bearded corn alone,
Let first the Atlantid Pleiads come to their morning setting
And the blazing star of the Cretan Crown sink in the sky,
Before you commit to the furrows the seed you owe them, before
You entrust the hope of the year to an earth that is still reluctant.
Many begin to sow before the setting of Maia,
But empty-eared is the harvest and laughs at all their hopes.
If vetch you care to sow, or the common kidney-bean,
And if you don't look down on the care of Egyptian lentil,
Boötes setting will give you a clear signal for this:
Begin, and go on sowing up to midwinter frosts.
    Wherefore the golden sun commands an orbit measured
In fixed divisions through the twelvefold signs of the universe.
Five zones make up the heavens: one of them in the flaming
Sun glows red for ever, for ever seared by his fire:
Round it to right and left the furthermost zones extend,
Blue with cold, ice-bound, frozen with black blizzards:
Between these and the middle one, weak mortals are given
Two zones by the grace of God, and a path was cut through both
Where the slanting signs might march and countermarch. The world,
Rising steeply to Scythia and the Riphaean plateaux,
Slopes down in the south to Libya.
This North pole's always above us: the South appears beneath
The feet of darkling Styx, of the deep-down Shadow People.
Here the great Snake glides out with weaving, elastic body

Writhing riverwise around and between the two Bears—
The Bears that are afraid to get wet in the water of Ocean.
At the South pole, men say, either it's dead of night,
Dead still, the shadows shrouded in night, blacked out for ever;
Or dawn returns from us thither, bringing the daylight back,
And when sunrise salutes us with the breath of his panting horses,
Down there eve's crimson star is lighting his lamp at last.
Hence we foreknow the weather of the uncertain sky,
The time to reap or sow,
The time that's best for lashing the treacherous sea with oars
And launching an armed fleet,
The proper time to throw the pine tree in the forest.
    Well for us that we watch the rise and fall of the sky-signs
And the four different seasons that divide the year equally.
Suppose the farmer is kept indoors by a spell of cold rain,
He can take his time about many jobs which later he'd have to
Scamp when the weather cleared: the ploughman hammers the hard tooth
Of the blunt plough: one chap will fashion troughs from a tree-trunk,
Another brand his cattle or number his sacks of grain.
Some sharpen stakes and forks,
Get ready ties of willow to bind the trailing vine.
Now you may weave light baskets from shoots of the bramble bush,
Dry your corn at the fire now and grind it down with a millstone.
Even on festival days some labours are allowed
By the laws of god and man: no religious scruple need stop you
From works of irrigation or hedging around your cornfield,
Bird-snaring, firing the brambles,
Dipping your bleating flock of sheep in the wholesome river.
Often its driver loads the flanks of the dawdling ass
With oil or with cheap apples, and returns from town later
Bearing a whetstone ready dressed or a lump of black pitch.

The moon herself has made some days in varying degrees
Lucky for work. Beware of the fifth: that is the birthday
Of Hell's pale king and the Furies; then earth spawned an unspeakable
Brood of titans and giants, gave birth to the ogre Typhoeus
And the brothers who leagued themselves to hack the heavens down:
Three times they tried, three times, to pile Ossa on Pelion —
Yes, and to roll up leafy Olympus on Ossa's summit;
And thrice our Father dislodged the heaped-up hills with a thunderbolt.
The seventeenth day is lucky both for setting a vine,
Roping and breaking steers, and fixing the loops on a loom.
The ninth is a good day for runaways, bad for burglars.
    Many things even go best in the raw night-hours or at sunrise
When the Dawn Star dews the earth.
By night it's best to mow light stubble, by night a meadow
That's parched, for a clammy moisture is always present at night-time.
A man there is who stays up late by winter firelight
With a penknife pointing torches;
Meanwhile, singing a song to lighten the lengthy task,
His wife runs through the loom with her shrill-rattling reed,
Or boils away on a fire the sweet liquid of wine-must
And skims with leaves the wave that foams in the shuddering kettle.
But the red-gold corn should always be cut in noonday heat,
In noonday heat the baked grain beat out on threshing-floor.
Plough and sow in the warm months, in your shirt-sleeves. Winter's an off-tim
For farmers: then they mostly enjoy their gains, hold jolly
Suppers amongst themselves.
Genial winter invites them and they forget their worries;
Just as, when ships in cargo have come to port at last,
Glad to be home the sailors adorn their poops with garlands.
Yet even now there's employment in season — acorns to gather
And berries off the bay tree, and olives, and blood-red myrtle:

Now you can lay your traps for the crane, your nets for the stag,
Go coursing long-eared hares, or whirl your hempen sling
To bring the fallow deer down —
Now when snow lies deep and streams jostle their pack-ice.

     Am I to tell you next of the storms and stars of autumn?
The things, when days draw in and summer's heat is abating,
That men must guard against? The dangers of showery spring,
When the prick-eared harvest already bristles along the plains
And when in the green blade the milky grain is swelling?
Well, often I've seen a farmer lead into his gloden fields
The reapers and begin to cut the frail-stalked barley,
And winds arise that moment, starting a free-for-all,
Tearing up by the roots whole swathes of heavy corn
And hurling them high in the air: with gusts black as a hurricane
The storm sent flimsy blades and stubble flying before it.
Often, too, huge columns of water come in the sky
And clouds charged off the deep amass for dirty weather
With rain-squalls black: then the whole sky gives way, falls,
Floods with terrific rain the fertile crops and the labours
Of oxen; filled are the ditches, dry rivers arise in spate
Roaring, the sea foams and seethes up the hissing fjords.
The Father, enthroned in midnight cloud, hurls from a flashing
Right hand his lightning: the whole
Earth trembles at the shock; the beasts are fled, and human
Hearts are felled in panic throughout the nations: on Athos ,
Rhodope or the Ceraunian massif his bolt flares down:
The south wind doubles its force and thicker falls the rain:
Now wail the woods with that gale tremendous, now the shores wail.
Fearing this, keep track of the signs and constellations,
Notice whither the cold star of Saturn takes himself
And into what sky-circles Mercury is moving.

           [Lines 307-337]

Above all, worship the gods, paying your yearly tribute
To the Corn-goddess — a sacrifice on the cheerful grass
Just at the close of winter, when spring has cleared the sky.
Oh then the lambs are fat, then are wines most mellow,
Sweet then is sleep and rich on mountains lie the shadows.
Let all your labouring men worship the Corn-goddess;
For her let the honeycomb be steeped in milk and mild wine,
The mascot led three times round the young crops — a victim
Fêted by all your fellows accompanying it in a body:
Let them call her into their houses
With a shout, and let nobody lay his sickle to the ripe corn
Till in her honour he's placed on his head a wreath of oak leaves
And danced impromptu dances and sung the harvester's hymn.

    So that we might be able to predict from manifest signs
These things — heatwaves and rain and winds that bring cold weather,
The Father himself laid down what the moon's phases should mean,
The cue for the south wind's dropping, the sign that often noted
Should warn a farmer to keep his cattle nearer the shippon.
At once, when winds are rising,
The sea begins to fret and heave, and a harsh crackling
Is heard from timbered heights, or a noise that carries far
Comes confused from the beaches, and copses moan crescendo.
At such a time are the waves in no temper to bear your curved ship —
A time when gulls are blown back off the deepsea flying
Swift and screeching inland, a time when cormorants
Play on dry land, and the heron
Leaves his haunt in the fens to flap high over the cloud.
Another gale-warning often is given by shooting stars
That streak downsky and blaze a trail through the night's blackness
Leaving a long white wake:
Often light chaff and fallen leaves eddy in the air,

Or feathers play tig skimming along the skin of water.
But when lightning appears from the quarter of the grim north wind,
When it thunders to south or west, then all the countryside
Is a-swim with flooded dykes and all the sailors at sea
Close-reef their dripping sails. No, rain need never take us
Unawares: for high-flying cranes will have flown to valley bottoms
To escape the rain as it rises, or else a calf has looked up
At the sky and snuffed the wind with nostrils apprehensive,
Or the tittering swallow has flitted around and around the lake,
And frogs in the mud have croaked away at their old complaint.
Often too from her underground workings the emmet, wearing
A narrow path, bears out her eggs; a giant rainbow
Bends down to drink; rook armies desert their feeding-ground
In a long column, wing-tip to wing-tip, their wings whirring.
Now seabirds after their kind, and birds that about Caÿster's
Asian waterflats grub in the fresh pools, zestfully fling
Showers of spray over their shoulders,
Now ducking their heads in the creeks, scampering now at the wavelets,
Making a bustle and frivolous pantomime of washing.
Then the truculent raven full-throated announces rain
As she stalks alone on the dry sand.
Even at night can girls, spinning their wool, be aware
That a storm approaches, for then they behold in the burning lamp
The oil sputter and crumbly mould collect on the wick.

    No less easy it is to foretell after rainy weather
Sun and unclouded skies, and by sure indications to know them.
Then, neither do star rays look blurred nor will the moon rise
As though she owed her light to the beams of her brother sun,
Nor lank and fleecy clouds be drawn across the heaven:
Kingfishers then, the pets of the Sea-goddess, will not preen their
Plumage along the shore in the warm sun, nor will gross

[Lines 369-399]

Swine remember to root and toss with their snouts the bed-straw.
Rather do mists hang low and crouch along the plain,
And the little owl, perched on a gable, watching the sun go down,
Keeps at her crazy night-call.
Aloft in the lucid air Nisus, a sparrowhawk,
Appears, and Scylla pays for that purple hair she stole:
Wherever in flight she parts the thin air with her lark's wing,
Look! her enemy, cruel, down the wind loudly whistling,
Nisus follows her close; where Nisus zooms upwind,
Frantic in flight she parts the thin air with her lark's wing.
Then rooks, the guttural talkers, three times or four repeat
A clear cool note, and often up there in the treetop cradles
Charmed by some unfamiliar sweet impulse we cannot guess at
Gossip among the leaves: they love, when rain is over,
To visit again their baby brood, their darling nests.
It's not, to my belief, that God has given them
A special instinct, or Fate a wider foreknowledge of things;
But, when the weather's changing, when the wet atmosphere
Shifts and a sky dripping from the south wind condenses
What was rare just now and rarefies what was condensed,
New images possess their mind, impulses move
Their heart other than moved them while the wind was herding the clouds.
Thus, the countryside over, begins that bird-chorale,
Beasts rejoice, and rooks caw in their exultation.
　　If you observe the hotfoot sun and the moon's phases,
To-morrow will never cheat you
Nor will you be taken in by the trick of a cloudless night.
When first at the new moon her radiance is returning,
If she should clasp a dark mist within her unclear crescent,
Heavy rain is in store for farmer and fisherman:
But if a virgin blush covers her face, there'll be

Some wind — wind always flushes the face of the golden moon.
And if at her fourth rising (this is a sign infallible)
She walk the heaven in purity of light, her horns not blurred,
All that day and the days
Which follow to the month's end you'll fear no rain or wind,
And sailors ashore shall pay their vows for a safe return to
Glaucus and Panope and Melicertes son of Ino.
The sun also at dawning and when he sinks in the deep
Will give you signs: his signs are the most reliable of all,
Both those he brings in the morning and those at the stars' ascending.
When at dawn he's dappled
With spots, concealed behind cloud, and half his orb is hidden,
You may look out for showers; for a southerly gale off the sea
Is driving, that means no good to trees or crops or cattle.
But when, towards daybreak, his beams filter between
Thick cloud, rayed out like spokes, or when the dawn arises
Pale from the saffron bed of Tithonus, then I fear
Vine-leaves will give your ripening grapes but poor protection —
Such a storm of harsh hail is coming to rattle and bounce on the roofs.
This too, when he's traversed the sky and is now declining,
Is of even more advantage to remember: — we often see
Various colours passing over his countenance;
The dark-green stands for rain, flame colour foretells an east wind;
But, should stains begin to be mixed with a ruddy fire,
Both wind and rain are brewing and you'll see them boiling over.
No one on such a night
Could induce me to cross the sea or even cast off my moorings.
But if, when he brings a dayspring and when he buries that day,
His orb is equally clear, you need not worry for rain-clouds,
Since you'll be watching the forests wave in a fine north wind.
Lastly, what the late evening conveys, from whence the wind drives

[Lines 431-461]

Fine-weather clouds, and what the damp south wind is brooding,
The sun discloses. Who dares call the sun a liar?
Often too he warns you of lurking imminent violence,
Of treachery, and wars that grow in the dark like a cancer.
The sun, when Caesar fell, had sympathy for Rome —
That day he hid the brightness of his head in a rusty fog
And an evil age was afraid his night would last for ever:
Though at that time the earth as well, the waves of the sea,
Mongrels and birds morose
Gave tongue to the doom. How often we saw Mount Aetna deluge
The fields of the Cyclops with lava from her cracked furnaces,
Rolling up great balls of flame and molten rocks!
In Germany they heard a clash of fighting echo
Through the whole sky: the Alps shook with unnatural shudders.
Likewise in stilly woods a voice was heard by many —
A monster voice, and phantoms miraculously pale
Were met at the dusk of night, and cattle spoke — an omen
Unspeakable! Rivers stopped, earth gaped, and ivories
In temples wept sad tears and brazen images sweated.
Po, the king of rivers, in maniac spate whirled round
Forests, washed them away, swept all over the plains
Herds and their byres together. A time it was when the guts of
Woe-working victims never failed to reveal the worst
Nor wells to seep with blood
Nor high-built cities to sound all night with the wolves' howling.
Never elsewhere have lightnings flickered so constantly
In a clear sky, or baleful comets burned so often.
Thus it ensued that Philippi's field saw Roman armies
Once again engaged in the shock of civil war;
And the High Ones did not think it a shame that we should twice
Enrich with our blood Emathia and the broad plains of Haemus.

[Lines 462-492]   18

Surely the time will come when a farmer on those frontiers
Forcing through earth his curved plough
Shall find old spears eaten away with flaky rust,
Or hit upon helmets as he wields the weight of his mattock
And marvel at the heroic bones he has disinterred.
O Gods of our fathers, native Gods, Romulus, Vesta
Who mothers our Tuscan Tiber and the Roman Palatine,
At least allow our young prince to rescue this shipwrecked era!
Long enough now have we
Paid in our blood for the promise Laomedon broke at Troy.
Long now has the court of heaven grudged you to us, Caesar,
Complaining because you care only for mortal triumphs.
For Right and Wrong are confused here, there's so much war in the world,
Evil has so many faces, the plough so little
Honour, the labourers are taken, the fields untended,
And the curving sickle is beaten into the sword that yields not.
There the East is in arms, here Germany marches:
Neighbour cities, breaking their treaties, attack each other:
The wicked War-god runs amok through all the world.
So, when racing chariots have rushed from the starting-gate,
They gather speed on the course, and the driver tugs at the curb-rein
—His horses runaway, car out of control, quite helpless.

BOOK TWO

BOOK TWO

So far I have sung the tillage of earth, the lore of heaven:
Now it's the turn of wine, and with it the trees that crowd
In woody copse, and the produce of the gradual-growing olive.
Come, Lord of the wine-press — everything here is lavish
By your largesse, for you the field's aflower and laden
With bins of autumn, the vintage foams in vats overflowing —
Come then, Lord of the wine-press, pull off your boots and paddle
Bare-legged with me and dye your shins purple in the grape juice!
     To begin. Nature is catholic in the propagation of trees.
Some without human help
Spring of their own sweet will and spread abroad by winding
Streams and on plains — soft osier, the bending Spanish broom,
Poplars, and the pale willow that shows a silver-blue leaf:
Again, some grow from seed they have dropped—the high-tiered chestnut,
The common oak, most prolific of leaf among woodland trees,
And the oak that in Greece they fancy is able to tell their fortune.
Others, like elm and cherry, have a thick undergrowth
Cropping up from their roots: the Parnassian bay-tree also,
When tiny, shelters beneath the immense shade of its mother.
Nature gave from the start such modes to evolve the green of
Each tribe of trees in forest, shrubbery, sacred wood.
Others we've found by experience.
One man takes suckers off the tender stock of the mother
And plants them in trenches: another fixes sets in the field
By notching stakes cross-wise or sharpening the wood to a point.
Some forest trees there are prefer the pinned-down arches
Of the layer, that make a nursery alive in the parent's earth.

23   [Lines 1-27]

Some need no root, and the pruner
Can safely commit to the soil cuttings from off a high branch.
What's more — and this is a marvel — if you take a saw to the trunk of
An olive, a root will come pushing out from the dry wood.
Often again we observe the boughs of one tree change
Without harm into another's — grafted apples growing
On a pear, and stony cherries reddening upon a plum tree.

So come, you countrymen, learn the correct training of each
In its kind, domesticate wild fruits by your cultivation,
And let not the earth be lazy ! It's good to plant with vines
Ismarus, and to clothe in olives Mount Taburnus.
And you, be at hand, and help me complete the task I've begun —
My pride, who rightfully share the chief of my renown —
My friend, and unfurl your flying sails for the sea lies open.
I cannot hope to include everything in my poem,
No, not if I'd a hundred tongues, a hundred mouths
And a voice like iron. But come and coast the shore: dry land
Is near: I'll not detain you
With lengthy preambles, digressions, or any poetic fiction.

Trees that spontaneously reach up to the world of light
Bear no fruit, it's true, but they grow up bonny and strong,
For natural vigour is in their soil. Yet even these, if
You graft on them or transplant them into prepared trenches,
Will cast their wildwood ways, and by constant cultivation
Be disciplined soon to whatever habits you design for them.
Even a barren sucker that shoots from the bottom of a tree
Will do the same, if you plant it out in open ground:
Otherwise, the leaves and boughs of its mother blanket it
From above, stifle its growth, dry up its fruitfulness.
A tree that springs from dropped seed
Grows slowly, it'll give shade one day to your descendants:

Apples deteriorate, losing their pristine savour,
And the vine bears nasty grapes that are good for nothing but birds.
The fact is, all of these require attention, all
Must be forced into furrows and tamed with much expense of labour.
Olives will answer best to truncheons, vines to the layer,
Myrtles to solid sets:
From slips you propagate the hardwood hazel, the huge
Ash, the shady poplar—the crown of Hercules,
And Jupiter's oaks; so too the palm that scales the sky
Is reared, and the fir that goes to take its chance at sea.
But the rugged arbutus is ingrafted from off the walnut,
And barren planes have carried a hearty crop of apples,
Chestnuts have borne beech-mast, the mountain ash blown white
With pear blossom, and pigs munched acorns under an elm tree.

     Grafting and budding are two different operations.
Where buds push out from the bark
And burst their delicate sheaths, you should make a narrow slit
In the actual knot: it's here that you enclose a bud
From another tree and train it to grow in the sappy rind.
Grafting's different—it's done by cutting a smooth trunk,
Splitting the wood deeply with wedges, and then inserting
The fertile scion: before long
That tree ascends to heaven in a wealth of happy branches,
Surprised at its changeling leaves and the fruits that are not its own.

     Next, there's more than a single species of hardy elms,
Of the willow, the nettle tree, or the cypresses of Ida;
More than one variety of fat olives you'll find—
Orchites, the raggaria, and the bitter-berried posea:
Many sorts of apples there are in orchards; the same branch
Bears not the Crustumine pear, the bergamot and the pound-pear.
Different the vintage grapes that trail on our own trees

[Lines 59-89]

From those you gather in Lesbos off a Methymnian vine.
Thasian and white Mareotic
Vines there are, one suited to heavy soil, one to light soil;
Psythian are best for raisin wine, while thin Lagean
On its day will trip your feet and tie your tongue in a knot.
There's the purple grape and the early. What poem can do justice
To Rhaetian? Yet even this cannot compete with Falernian.
Amminean vines afford us the most full-bodied wine,
To which must yield the Tmolian and even the royal Chian
And lesser Argite — though none other can rival the latter
For sheer abundance or length of time it remains at its best.
I'm not forgetting Rhodian wine, by gods and festive
Mortals highly esteemed, or the bountiful grapes of Bumastus.
But to catalogue all the wines and their names would be quite beyond me
And serve no useful purpose:
If you wish to know their number, go and tot up the grains
Of sand that are whirled around by a sand-storm in the Sahara,
Or count the waves that break along Adriatic coasts
When an easterly gale comes down in gusts upon the shipping.
     Now different plants will need different soils for their nurture.
Willows grow by streams, alders in soggy marshland;
The barren rowan tree is found on rocky hillsides;
Myrtles crowd to the sea-coast:
Vines love an open hill, yews a cold northerly aspect.
Consider the ends of the earth and those who cultivate them—
Arabs away in the east, Ukrainians in their woad:
No less widespread are the homes of trees. India alone
Gives ebony, Arabia the tree of frankincense.
Need I tell you about the balsam that distils
From fragrant wood, or the globes of evergreen gum-arabic?
The soft cotton that glimmers in plantations of Ethiopia?

The way the Chinese comb the delicate silk from their leaves?
Then there's the Indian jungle that borders Ocean, just
In the furthest corner of the world: no arrow can reach its tree-tops
However hard they shoot — and the Indians, I assure you,
Aren't fools at archery.
Persia gives us the peart juice and the lingering taste
Of citron, a favoured fruit, and one that will come in handy
If ever an unkind stepmother puts anything in your cup —
Poisonous herbs, for instance, mixed with malignant cantrips —
As an antidote to drive the toxin out of your system.
The tree itself is big, very like a bay in appearance:
Indeed, were it not for the different perfume it wafts abroad,
A bay it was: the leaves won't fall in any wind,
The flower is most tenacious: this tree is used by the Medes
To sweeten a stinking breath and to cure old men of asthma.

But neither the Median forests, that rich land, nor fair Ganges,
Nor Hermus rolling in gold
Compares with Italy — no, not Bactra nor the Indies
Nor all Arabia's acres of spice-enrichened soil.
This land of ours has never been ploughed by bulls fire-breathing
Nor sown with dragon's teeth;
It has never known a harvest of serried helmeted spearmen:
Rather is it a country fulfilled with heavy corn and
Campanian wine, possessed by olives and prosperous herds.
Here the charger gallops onto the plain in his pride,
Here the white-fleeced flocks and the bull, a princely victim
Washed over and over in Clitumnus' holy water,
Head our Roman triumphs to the temples of the gods.
Here is continual spring and a summer beyond her season;
Cattle bear twice yearly, apples a second crop.
No bloodthirsty tigers are found here, no fierce young lions roar,

[Lines 121-151]

No monkshood grows to deceive and poison the wretch who picks it,
Nor does the scaly snake slither at such great length
On the ground or gather himself into so many coils here.
Number our noble cities and all the works of our hands,
The towns piled up on toppling cliffs, the antique walls
And the rivers that glide below them.
Must I commemorate the Upper sea and the Lower?
The lakes so great? Lake Larius the greatest of them all,
Lake Benacus that tosses and growls like a little ocean?
Shall I mention our harbours, the mole that was built to bar the Lucrine
And made the deep cry out in mighty indignation
Where the Sound of Julius murmurs with the noise of the sea locked out
And Tyrrhene tides flow through a canal into Averno?
Veins of silver and copper Italy too has revealed
And rivers running with gold.
Active her breed of men — the Marsians and Sabellians,
Ligurians used to hardship, Volscian javelin-throwers;
Mother she is of the Decii, Marii, great Camilli,
The Scipio's relentless in war; and of you, most royal Caesar,
Who now triumphant along the furthest Asian frontiers
Keep the war-worthless Indians away from the towers of Rome.
Hail, great mother of harvests! O land of Saturn, hail!
Mother of Men! For you I take my stand on our ancient
Glories and arts, I dare to unseal the hallowed sources
And sing a rural theme throughout the cities of Rome.
    Now it is time to deal with the nature of different soils,
The strength and colour of each, their quotient of fertility.
First, a stubborn soil and inhospitable hills,
Where the clay is lean and the fields are strewn with stones and brushwood,
Delight in the long-lived olive.
You'll know such soil by the wealth of wild olives that grow

All over it and litter the ground with their wild berries.
But where the soil is rich and rejoices in sweet moisture,
Or a level expanse grown deep with grass all lush and verdant,
Such as we often find when we look down into a fold
Of the hollow hills (for becks flow hither bearing alluvial
Soil from the heights above), or an upland facing south
Where the plough is baulked by bracken: —
Such sites as these one day will produce superlative vines,
Robust and in wine abundant; generous givers of the grape
And of that juice we pour to the gods from a golden chalice
While the plump Etruscan plays his ivory flute at the altar
And platters bend with the weight of the smoking sacrifice.
    But if your business be rather the keeping of calves and cattle,
The breeding of sheep, or goats that burn up all growing things,
You should try the woodland pastures and the prairies of rich Tarentum
And plains such as unlucky Mantua has lost
Where snow-white swans among the river weeds are feeding:
Here neither springs of water nor grass will fail your flocks,
And all that the cattle consume
In a long day is restored by the cool dew during the short night.
    As a rule, soil that is black and turns up right at the pressure
Of the ploughshare, or crumbling soil (for this we reproduce
By ploughing) is best for corn: no other plain will yield you
So many waggonloads drawn home by the slow-gait oxen.
Or acres from which the ploughman has carted the wood away:
Intolerant of trees that stood idle for many a year,
He felled them, root and branch he demolished the ancient dwellings
Of birds; their nests abandoned, the birds have made for the sky,
But the land that once was wild is gleaming now with furrows.
In hill-country you'll get gravel, a hungry soil
That gives the bees a bare subsistence of spurge and rosemary:

[Lines 183-213]

Friable stone and chalk is where the black snakes burrow
Finding no land its like
For dainty food and the tunnelling of their serpentine retreats.
Land that is breathing out lank mist and volatile vapours,
That drinks the moisture up or sweats it away at will
And wears an evergreen garment made of its own grasses
And does not affect your implements with salty, scurfy rust—
That land will prove a winner at winding your elms with vines
And yielding olive oil: just try that land and you'll find it
A masterpiece for grazing, a meek one for the plough.
Such land they farm round Capua, in the country beside Vesuvius,
And where the floods of the Clanius have emptied old Acerrae.
 Now let me tell you how to distinguish the various soils.
If you wish to know whether soil is loose or uncommonly stiff
(For corn requires the one and vineyards thrive on the other—
Compact soil suiting the former, a loose-knit one the latter),
First mark a place with your eye and have a pit sunk deep
In the solid ground, then put all the earth back again
And stamp it level on top:
If it fails to fill up the cavity, that soil is loose and fitted
For pasture and generous vines: but if you cannot replace
It all, and earth is left over after you've filled the pit,
That land is of close texture; look out for clinging clods there—
A sticky glebe that'll need your strongest oxen to plough it.
Salty land, again, and land as they say that is 'sour'
(No catch for corn, to be sweetened by no amount of ploughing,
Where vines lose quality and orchards their reputation)
You'll detect by this experiment: — take down from your smoky rafters
Baskets of plaited withies and the strainers used in a wine-press;
Fill them up with that nasty soil and fresh spring-water
And tread them well together:

[Lines 214-244]   30

The water will all strain off in large drops through the withies,
But the bitter taste of it will show as plain as a pikestaff
On the face of the taster, twisting it into a sour grimace.
Further, soil that is fat and rich will answer briefly
To the following test: when tossed in the hand it never crumbles
But adheres to the fingers, like pitch growing stickier in the handling.
Damp ground encourages rank vegetation; by nature it runs
To freakish growth. Preserve me from land that is over-fertile
And proves itself too strong by a precocious corn-crop!
Weigh the soil in your hand and it gives you a quiet hint
Whether it's light or heavy: you'll learn at a glance that it's black
Or whatever colour it may be. But to find the damnable cold soil
Is difficult: only Corsican pines and poisonous yew trees
At times betray it, or sprawling ivy offers a clue.

  Bearing in mind these rules, remember to give your land
Plenty of sun, and trench the broad hillsides, and turn
Your clods to welcome the north wind,
Long before you plant your vines. Best are the fields
Where soil is crumbly: winds and hard frosts take care of that,
And a deal of hard digging to stir and loosen the acres.
But if a man intends to take extra precaution,
He'll choose a similar soil both for his seedlings' nursery
And for the vineyard where they are soon to be planted out,
Lest the young slips find their foster-mother unsympathetic.
What's more, he may even carve on the bark four points of the compass
So that, when a plant is transferred, it shall turn the same face
To north or south as it turned
From birth: so important are habits developed in early days.

  Find out first if your vines are better laid out upon
Hilly or level ground. When you're plotting out rich plain-land,
Sow thickly: a thick-set vineyard is no more backward in bearing.

[Lines 245-275]

On ground that is broken by tumps and on the recumbent hills
Give your rows more elbow-room; but see that the alleys
Of trees are planted there in squares with equal precision:
Just as in war when a legion deploys by companies
From column of route into line across an open plain,
And the ranks are dressed by the right, and the earth all undulates
With flashing bronze, and the battle
Waits while the War-god saunters uncertain between the armies.
Let all be spaced out in alleys of perfect symmetry,
Not merely so that their vistas may charm a frivolous mind,
But because only thus can earth supply impartial
Vigour to all, and the growing boughs have room to extend.

        You will ask me perhaps what depth you ought to dig your trenches.
The vine I'd venture to plant in quite a shallow one:
But trees should be set deeper, well down in the earth's heart —
The oak above all, that raises
Her head as far into heaven as her roots go down towards hell:
Wherefore no storms, no gusts, no rains can ever uproot her,
But immovable she remains
Outlasting children's children through centuries of human life.
Far and wide she stretches her boughs, her steadfast arms —
A central column upholding that heavy spread of shade.

        Avoid sloping your vineyard towards the setting sun,
And planting hazel among the vines. Never take the highest
Vine-shoots, nor tear your cuttings from off the top of a tree
(Such is earth's attraction, the lower do best), nor with blunt blade
Wound the young vines. Don't plant wild olive to support your vines:
For often it happens some careless shepherd lets fall a spark
That, smouldering furtively under their resinous bark at first,
Gets a grip on the wood, leaps out on the leaves aloft,
And roars at the sky; rears up then

In triumph over the branches and crests of the trees, their master,
Rolling the whole plantation in flame, heavenward heaving
A cloud of smoke gross-bodied, greasy and black as pitch —
And worse still if a storm bears down on the wood to marshal
The flames and fan them afar. Should this befall, your vines
Are dead to the roots; you may cut them away, but they'll not recover
Nor awake in green from the earth below as once they did:
Wild olives alone will live there, a barren, bitter stock.

  Let no one, however canny, induce you to work your land
When it's bone-hard under a north wind.
Then icy winter closes down the countryside —
You may cast your seed, but the numb root will never take hold on earth.
The time for setting vines is the first flush of spring
When that white bird arrives, the stork, the bane of serpents;
Or the first frosts of autumn, days when the hotfoot sun
Is not on winter's verge yet, but summer is now passing.
Oh, spring is good for leaves in the spinney, good to forests,
In spring the swelling earth aches for the seed of new life.
Then the omnipotent Father of air in fruitful showers
Comes down to his happy consort
And greatly breeds upon her great body manifold fruit.
Then are the trackless copses alive with the trilling of birds,
And the beasts look for love, their hour come round again:
Lovely the earth in labour, under a tremulous west wind
The fields unbosom, a mild moisture is everywhere.
Confident grows the grass, for the young sun will not harm it;
The shoots of the vine are not scared of a southerly gale arising
Or the sleety rain that slants from heaven beneath a north wind,—
No, bravely now they bud and all their leaves display.
So it was, I believe, when the world first began,
Such the illustrious dawning and tenor of their days.

    [Lines 307-337]

It was springtime then, great spring
Enhanced the earth and spared it the bitter breath of an east wind—
A time when the first cattle lapped up the light, and men
Children of earth themselves arose from the raw champaign,
And wild things issued forth in the wood, and stars in the sky.
How could so delicate creatures endure the toil they must,
Unless between cold and heat there came this temperate spell
And heaven held the earth in his arms and comforted her?

To proceed: whatever plantations you're setting down on your land,
Spread rich dung and be careful to cover with plenty of earth:
Dig in some porous stones or rough shells at their roots
Through which the rain-water may trickle and evaporate again
And the plants perk up their spirits.
Men have been known ere now to lay a rock above them
Or a weighty potsherd—protection against a flooding rain,
When heatwave comes with the Dog Star and cracks the fields with thirst.

Once you have set the seedlings, it remains to loosen the soil
Thoroughly at their roots, and ply the heavy hoe;
To discipline the soil with deep-pressed plough, and steer
Your straining oxen up and down the alleys of the vineyard.
Then make ready and fit smooth reeds, poles of peeled wood,
Ash stakes for the forked uprights,
Upon whose strength your vines can mount and be trained to clamber
Up the high-storied elm trees, not caring tuppence for wind.

As long as your vines are growing in first and infant leaf,
They're delicate, need indulgence. And while the gay shoots venture
Heavenward, given their head and allowed to roam the sky,
Don't use a knife upon them yet—a fingernail
Is enough for pruning their leaves and thinning them out in places.
But when they've shot up and are holding the elms in strong embrace,
Dock the leaves, lop the branches:

[Lines 338-368]   34

Till now they could not bear the steel; now you must show them
Greater severity, curbing their frisky wanton growth.
    There's hedging, too, to be done: every kind of beast you must bar,
Especially while the vine-leaf is young and inexperienced.
For, beside cruel winters and bullying suns, the woodland
Buffalo and restless hunting roedeer habitually
Make a playground there, and sheep and greedy heifers a pasture.
White frosts that stiffen all
And heat of summer that lies so heavy on scorching crags
Hurt a vineyard less than flocks with their venomous teeth
And the scars they leave on the nibbled stems will damage it.
This accounts for the sacrifice of a goat to the Wine-god
On every altar, the staging of the ancient ritual plays,
The prizes that round their hamlets and crossroads the Athenians
Gave for local talent, when they danced on the greasy wine-skins
Junketing in the meadows and jolly in their cups.
The Ausonians, too, settlers from Troy, are accustomed to hold a
Beano, their poems unpolished and unrestrained their jokes:
They wear the most hideous wooden
Masks, and address the Wine-god in jovial ditties, and hang
Wee images of the god to sway from windy pine-boughs.
Thus will every vine advance to full fruition
And valleys will teem and dells and dingles and combes deep-wooded—
Yes, wherever the Wine-god has turned his handsome head.
So let us duly pay to that god the homage we owe him
In anthems our fathers sang, in offerings of fruit and cake:
Led by the horn, let the ritual goat be stood at the altar,
And the rich meat of the sacrifice roast upon hazel spits.
    Another task there is, the dressing of vines, that is never
Finished: for year by year
Three times, four times you should loosen the soil: you cannot turn

[Lines 369-399]

And break the clods with your hoe too often; the whole plantation's
Load of shade must be lightened. A farmer's work proceeds in
Cycles, as the shuttling year returns on its own track.
And now, the time when a vineyard puts off its reluctant leaves
And a bitter north wind has blown away the pride of the woodland,
Even now the countryman actively pushes on to the coming
Year and its tasks; attacking the naked vine with a curved
Pruning-knife, he shears and trims it into shape.
Be the first to dig the land, the first to wheel off the prunings
For the bonfire, the first to bring your vine-poles under cover;
But the last to gather the vintage. Twice will the vines grow thick
With shade, and twice will a tangle of briars overrun the vineyards;
Each makes for hard work: so admire a large estate if you like,
But farm a small one. Further,
You'll find rough broom in the woods and reeds on the river bank
To be cut, and the willow beds will give you plenty of work.
Now the vines are tied, the plants are done with pruning,
The last vine-dresser sings over his finished labours,
Yet still you must keep the soil busy, the dust on the move,
And watch apprehensive for weather which threatens the ripening grape.
    Olives are just the opposite: they require no cultivation
And have no use for the sickle knife or the stiff-tooth rake
Once they've dug themselves in on the fields and stood up to winds.
Earth herself, by the crooked plough laid bare, provides
Moisture enough for the plants and a heavy crop from the ploughshare.
Thus shall you breed the rich olive, beloved of Peace.
    Orchards too, when once they have tasted the power in their trunks
And realized their own strength, race up to the stars by nature
Needing no help from us.
No less does the wildwood also come out with fruits galore.
And blood-red berries like rubies adorn the untilled bird-land.

There's clover to be cut, firewood gleaned in the forest:
Night-long the fires are fed, and their light is pooled around.
Do men still hesitate to sow and take some trouble?

    Why should I stick to big trees? Willow and humble broom
Give plenty of leaf to cattle and shade enough for a shepherd,
Hedges they make for crops and a feed for the honey-bee.
Pleasant it is to behold the box trees wave on Cytorus,
Groves of Narycian pine, fields under no obligation
To man or his implements.

    Even the fruitless forests you find on peaks of Caucasus,
For ever torn and tossed by the storm-breathing east wind,
Yield each a special product — pine wood that's used in shipyards,
Cedar and cypress wood that go to the building of houses.
From wood the countryman turns the spokes for wheels and the waggon's
Solid wheels, and wooden the keels you lay down for ships.
Willows provide our withies, elms leaf-fodder for cattle,
But myrtle bears tough spear-shafts, cornel your cavalry-lances
Good in battle, while bows from Iturean yew are fashioned.
Smooth lime and box which the lathe
Has shaved take shape as well, are chamfered with sharp chisels.
The alder too, when you launch it upon the Po, rides lightly
That boiling stream; while bees are used to hide their swarms
Within some hollow bark or the heart of a rotten ilex.
What has the Wine-god given so thoroughly worth our thanks?
Much, indeed, he has done deserving blame. It was he
Who maddened and killed the Centaurs, and Rhoetus and Pholus, and made
Hylaeus brawl and go for the Lapithae with a bottle.

    Oh, too lucky for words, if only he knew his luck,
Is the countryman who far from the clash of armaments
Lives, and rewarding earth is lavish of all he needs!
True, no mansion tall with a swanky gate throws up

[Lines 431-461]

In the morning a mob of callers to crowd him out and gape at
Doorposts inlaid with beautiful tortoiseshell, attire
Of gold brocade, connoisseur's bronzes.
No foreign dyes may stain his white fleeces, nor exotic
Spice like cinnamon spoil his olive oil for use:
But calm security and a life that will not cheat you,
Rich in its own rewards, are here: the broad ease of the farmlands,
Caves, living lakes, and combes that are cool even at midsummer,
Mooing of herds, and slumber mild in the trees' shade.
Here are glades game-haunted,
Lads hardened to labour, inured to simple ways,
Reverence for God, respect for the family. When Justice
Left earth, her latest footprints were stamped on folk like these.

    Since Poetry for me comes first — my goddess and chief delight
Whose devotee I am, with a master-passion adoring —
I wish above all she accept me, revealing the stars and the sky-routes,
The several eclipses of the sun, the moon pallid in labour,
The cause of earthquakes and the force that compels the deepsea
To swell, to break all bounds, to fall back on itself again;
The reason why winter suns race on to dip in the ocean,
And what delays the long nights.
But if a sluggishness, a lack of heat in my heart's blood
Denies me access to these mysteries of the universe,
Then let the country charm me, the rivers that channel its valleys,
Then may I love its forest and stream, and let fame go hang.
Oh for the plain of Spercheus, Taÿgeta where the Spartan
Girls run mad! And oh for one to stay me in Haemus'
Cool glens, and comfort me in a world of branchy shade!
Lucky is he who can learn the roots of the universe,
Has mastered all his fears and fate's intransigence
And the hungry clamour of hell.

   [Lines 462-492]   38

But fortunate too the man who is friends with the country gods —
Pan and old Silvanus and the sisterhood of nymphs:
The fasces have no power to disturb him, nor the purple
Of monarchs, nor civil war that sets brother at brother's throat,
Nor yet the scheming Dacian as he marches down from the Danube,
Nor the Roman Empire itself and kingdoms falling to ruin.
He has no poor to pity, no envy for the rich.
The fruit on the bough, the crops that the field is glad to bear
Are his for the gathering: he spares not a glance for the iron
Rigour of law, the municipal racket, the public records.
Other men dare the sea with their oars blindly, or dash
On the sword, or insinuate themselves into royal courts:
One ruins a whole town and the tenements of the poor
In his lust for jewelled cups, for scarlet linen to sleep on;
One piles up great wealth, gloats over his cache of gold;
One gawps at the public speakers; one is worked up to hysteria
By the plaudits of senate and people resounding across the benches:
These shed their brothers' blood
Merrily, they barter for exile their homes beloved
And leave for countries lying under an alien sun.
    But still the farmer furrows the land with his curving plough:
The land is his annual labour, it keeps his native country,
His little grandsons and herds of cattle and trusty bullocks.
Unresting the year teems with orchard fruit, or young
Of cattle, or sheaves of corn,
Brimming the furrows with plenty, overflowing the barns.
Winter comes, when olives are crushed in the press, and pigs
Return elate with acorns, and woods give arbutus berries:
Autumn drops her varied fruits at our feet, while far
Above on sunny rocks the vintage basks and mellows.
And all the time he has dear children who dote on kisses,

[Lines 493-523]

A house that preserves the tradition of chastity, cows that hang
Their milky udders, and plump young goats on the happy green
Romping and butting with their horns.
The farmer himself keeps holidays when, at ease in a meadow,
A fire in the midst and friends there to crown the flowing bowl,
He drinks the health of the Wine-god and arranges for his herdsmen
A darts-match, setting up the target upon an elm tree,
And the labourers bare their sinewy bodies for country wrestling.
Such was the life the Sabines lived in days of old,
And Remus and his brother: so it was beyond all question
That Tuscany grew to greatness, Rome became queen of the world
Ringing her seven citadels with a single wall.
Before the rise of the Cretan
Lord, before impious men slaughtered bullocks for the banquet,
Such was the life that golden Saturn lived upon earth:
Mankind had not yet heard the bugle bellow for war,
Not yet heard the clank of the sword on the hard anvil. . . .

    But we have covered a deal of ground in our course, and now
It's time to slip off the harness from the necks of our reeking horses.

BOOK THREE

BOOK THREE

You too, great goddess of sheepfolds, I'm going to sing, and you
Apollo, a shepherd once, and the woods and streams of Arcadia.
Other themes, which might have pleasured an idle mind,
Are hackneyed all of them: everyone's heard of cruel
Eurystheus and the outrageous altar Busiris built.
Who does not know about Hylas, Latona who lived on Delos,
Hippodame and Pelops that horseman heroic, renowned
For his ivory shoulder? No, I must venture a theme will exalt me
From earth and give me wings and a triumph on every tongue.
If life enough is left me,
I'll be the first to bring the Muse of song to my birthplace
From Greece, and wear the poet's palm for Mantua;
And there in the green meadows I'll build a shrine of marble
Close to the waterside, where the river Mincius wanders
With lazy loops and fringes the banks with delicate reed.
Caesar's image shall stand there in the midst, commanding my temple,
While I, like a victor, conspicuous in crimson robes, shall drive
A hundred four-horse chariots up and down by the river.
All Greece will leave Alpheus and the Peloponnesian groves
To take part in the races and boxing-bouts I've arranged.
I myself, wearing a chaplet of trimmed olive,
Will present the prizes. How nice now
To lead the ritual walk to the shrine and watch the sacrifice,
Or to stare at the stage revealed when the scenes are shifted
And the crimson curtain rising embroidered with figures of Britons.
On the doors of my temple I'll have engraved in gold and solid
Ivory a battle scene — the Romans beating the Indians,

[Lines 1-27]

And here the enormous stream of Nile a-surge with a naval
Battle, and columns rising cast from the bronze of warships.
I'll add the cities of Asia we've mastered, Armenians routed,
Parthians whose forte is flight and shooting over their shoulder;
Two trophies taken in battle from different foes, a double
Triumph from either shore.
Parian stone shall stand there, breathing monuments—
The brood of Assaracus, our genealogy from Jove,
Tros our ancestor, and Apollo founder of Troy.
Envious men shall gaze in fear at the Furies, the pitiless
River of Hell, Ixion lashed with writhing snakes
To his giant wheel, and the rock that Sisyphus can't stop rolling.
Meanwhile let us pursue the woodland ways, the virgin
Lawns, my friend, the difficult task you have laid upon me.
Without your help, my spirit lacks high ambition. Come then,
Break up my lassitude! Loud is Cithaeron calling
And the hounds of Taÿgetus and Epidaurus tamer of horses,
And the woods all answer Yes and echo the call again.
Yet soon will I stir myself
To tell of Caesar's furious battles, to give him fame
For as many years as divide his day from the birth of Tithonus.

Suppose you covet the prize at Olympia and breed horses,
Or suppose you're breeding bullocks strong-bodied for the plough,
The chief thing is the choosing of dams. In a cow the following
Points should be looked for — a rough appearance, a coarse head,
Generous neck, and dewlaps hanging from jaw to leg;
Flanks as roomy as you like; everything built on a large scale,
Even the hoof; and shaggy ears under the crooked horns.
I have nothing against an animal of prominent white markings,
Or one that rejects the yoke and is hasty at times with her horn —
More like a bull to look at,

[Lines 28-58]   44

Tall all over, dusting the ground with her tail as she goes.
The proper period for a cow to mate and calve
Ends before the tenth, begins after the fourth year:
For the rest she is neither fit for breeding nor strong for ploughing.
Within these limits, while the herd is young and lusty,
Loose the males, early give over your cattle to love,
Keep up your stock by breeding from one to the next generation.
Of the measure of days allowed to piteous mortals, the best days
Are first to leave: illness and sorry old age loom up,
Suffering and death's untender mercies take all away.
Some beasts there will always be
That you wish to exchange: replace them, of course; and to compensate
For their loss, be quick to choose the young of the herd each year.
      Equal care must be exercised in the picking of horseflesh.
It's essential that those you wish to rear for stud should receive
Particular attention right from the very start.
Notice a thoroughbred foal in the paddock — how from birth
He picks his feet up high, stepping fastidiously;
First of the herd he'll venture onto the highroad, and ford
The menacing river, and brave the unknown dangers of bridges;
Nor will he shy at a meaningless noise. He shows a proud neck,
A finely tapering head, short barrel and fleshy back,
And his spirited chest ripples with muscle: (bays and roans
Are soundest, white or dun
Horses the worst). If he hears armour clang in the distance,
He can't keep still, the ears prick up, the limbs quiver,
He drinks the air, he jets it in hot steam out of his nostrils.
The mane is thick, and tumbles on the right shoulder when tossed:
The spine runs over the loins, sunk between two ridges;
The solid hoof makes a deep clatter and hurls up divots.
Such a horse was Cyllarus, that Pollux broke in; and such were

[Lines 59-89]

The two-yoke team of the War-god
And the horses of great Achilles, mentioned by Greek poets.
Such the guise that Saturn assumed to escape his wife,
A horse-mane streaming over his neck as he streaked away
And made the peaks of Pelion resound with a stallion's neighing.

Yet even that horse, when he weakens from illness or weight of years,
You must pension off and spare no pity for age's failings.
To be old is to be cold in rut, to prolong a loveless
Labour impotently; and whenever it comes to the conflict,
The flame is no more than a crackling of thorns, a foolish fury.
So mark them for youth and mettle
Above all: and next for other merits — their parents' pedigree,
The prizes and beatings they've taken, and how they've taken each.
Now look! It's a chariot race! They've charged from the starting-gate,
They're galloping down the course all out, they're covering the ground!
Each driver's hope runs high; his heart is drained with terror,
Drumming with mad excitement: the drivers whirling their whips,
Leaning forward, giving the horses their head, the hot wheels flying,
Now *ventre-à-terre* they seem to travel, and then bouncing
High to be twitched through the air and trying to soar on the breezes:
No slackening or respite: the course is a cloud of yellow dust,
The drivers are wet with the spindrift breath of the horses behind them.
So keen they are for the laurels, and victory means so much.
Erichthon thought of the four-horse
Chariot first, and rode a winning race on its wheels.
The Lapithae, celebrated horsemen, invented the bridle
And the training-ring: it was they who taught cavalrymen
The arts of the *haute école*.
Racers and chargers are both a job to breed: for either
It's youth, mettle and pace that trainers first demand —
No matter how often a horse may have charged and routed the foe,

No matter if he come from Epirus or brave Mycenae
Or trace his pedigree back even to Neptune's stable.

    Bearing in mind all this, they are forewarned and busy
To feed high and fill out with solid flesh the stallion
Whom they have chosen leader and bridegroom-lord of the herd:
They cut the flowering clover, they provide water and corn,
Lest the pleasured work be too much for him, and weakly sons
Prove the sire undernourished.
But the dams they deliberately keep hungry to fine them down;
And when the instinctive lust for mating first shall tease them,
They let them have no leaves and fence them away from water:
Often too they make them gallop and sweat in the sun
When threshing-floors groan heavily under the pounding flail
And empty chaff is wafted about on a freshening west wind.
This they do lest the breeding ground be dulled by indulgence,
The furrows clogged and inert
That should fasten thirstily on love and bury it far within.

    The care of the sires becomes less important now, and the dams
Need more attention. Their months are run, they are long in foal now:
Madness to yoke them and make them haul your heavy waggons,
To let them clear the road at a leap or gallop over
Meadows in breakneck flight or swim the racing rivers:
But rather let them feed in roomy meads, along
Full streams, where moss is growing and the bank most green with grass,
And caves give shelter and cliffs lean out in lengthening shadow.
About the groves of Silarus and Alburnus evergreen
In holm-oak swarms an insect
We call the gadfly ('oestrus' is the Greek name for it)—
A brute with a shrill buzz that drives whole herds crazy
Scattering through the woods, till sky and woods and the banks of
Bone-dry rivers are stunned and go mad with their bellowing.

[Lines 121-151]

Juno once, giving rein to horrible rage, decided
To plague with this pest the heifer-daughter of Inachus.
This fly, which is most ferocious in the heat of summer noons,
You must keep from your breeding cattle and bring the herd to pasture
When the sun's but newly risen or the stars are fetching the night.

    After birth, your care is all transferred to the calves:
At once you will brand the mark of their breed on those you wish
To rear for raising stock,
For sacrifice at the altar, or for tilling the soil
And turning the broken clods across the puckered plain.
The rest of the herd are put out to graze on the meadow grasses:
But those you would train for the practice and profit of agriculture
At a tender age you'll take in hand and set on the right road
Of discipline, while their mind is unformed, their youth docile.
First, tie around the neck a loose halter of light withy:
Next, when the neck that was free
Has bowed to bondage, use these same halters for yoking
Matched pairs of bullocks together, and make them walk in step:
Let them draw empty carts now, time and time again
Over the ground, and groove a light track in the dust:
After this may the beechen axle strain with a big load
Creaking, the linked wheels be drawn by the copper-edged shaft.
While they are yet unbroken, you'll cut for them not only
Hay and the fine leaves of the willow and fenny sedge,
But corn in the blade. Don't follow our forbears' custom, whereby
Mother-cows filled the snowy milk-pails: their young should have all
The benefit of their udders.

    But if your aim is rather to breed cavalry horses,
Or go in for chariot-racing at the Olympic games
Hurtling along by Alpheus in the grove of Jupiter's house,
First you will train the horse to watch the pride and panoply

Of regiments, to stand the bugle, or bear the squeal of
Dragging wheels and hear the jangle of harness in stable:
Then, little by little, the trainer wheedles him
To love a word of praise and the sound of his neck being patted.
This he may do when barely weaned, and try a rope-bit
In his mouth now and then
Though weak and wambling still, unaware of his growing power.
But when he's a three-year-old and his fourth summer is here,
Let him start presently to pace the ring and step
Harmoniously and learn to move at a limber stride
And begin to look like a worker. Then will he challenge the wind
To a race, and as if he were free of the rein fly over the open
Downs and leave but the lightest print of his hoof on the dust,
Like a north wind when from the frontiers of ice in gathering force
It swoops, drives helter-skelter the cold dry northern clouds:
The cornfields deep and the deepsea
Shudder with the gusts that flick them, and treetops in the forest
Cry aloud, and long rollers ride to the beach:
So flies that wind, sweeping field and flood as it goes.
Either that horse, sweating, mouth flecked with bloody foam,
Will last the distance at Elis and pass the finishing-post,
Or his pliant neck is better in harness pulling a curricle.
Then at last, when they're broken in, fill out their bodies
With coarse mixed mash: for until
You break them, their hearts are too high-flown, they jib at handling,
Refuse to bear the lash or obey the cruel curb.

But the most effective way to reinforce their strength
Is to bar them off from the passion and blinding goads of lust,
Whether your fancy is the breeding of bulls or horses.
Therefore they relegate the bull to a lonely pasture
Far away, railed off by a mountain and broad rivers,

49   [Lines 183-213]

Or to solitary confinement within the farm's rich stall.
For the female fritters away his strength and burns him up
With gazing at her, and makes him forget the woods and meadows —
So sweet her enticement — and often
Compels her proud lovers to fight it out with their horns.
A handsome heifer is grazing upon the slopes of Sila:
Two bulls begin to encounter furiously and inflict
Many gashes, until their bodies are dark with blood;
Their horns confront, lock with a crash and take the strain,
The forests and far-reaching skies roar back at them.
Nor is it the way of the fighters to herd together; the one
Defeated goes into retirement far off in unknown regions,
Groaning much at his own humiliation, the blows of
The cocky victor, the loss of a love not yet avenged;
He looks around his stall, then leaves that ancestral kingdom.
Therefore he trains assiduously, and lies untiring
On a makeshift bed among
Flint rocks, and feeds upon rough leaves and pointed reed-grass:
He practises putting all his fury into his horns
By goring trunks of trees, he butts at the air in anger,
He paws and tosses the sand as a prelude of coming battle.
Afterwards, his strength collected, his powers repaired,
He advances and hurtles headlong on the foe who has forgot him:
As when a wave begins to whiten out in mid-ocean
It draws a swelling curve far off from the deep, and landwards
Rolling roars tremendous among the rocks and falls
Like a hill, like the cliff it strikes, and the wave boils up from below
Eddying and hurls dark shingle high up along the shore.
　　All manner of life on earth — men, fauna of land and sea,
Cattle and coloured birds —
Run to this fiery madness: love is alike for all.

At no season but love's does the lioness so neglect
Her cubs and range so savage over the plain, or the clumsy
Bear deal out such wholesale death and destruction in the woods;
Then is the boar morose, the tigress in a wicked temper;
Ah, that's no time to be wandering alone through the Libyan desert!
Look how a horse shudders in his whole frame, if the familiar
Scent is but borne downwind!
Nothing will hold him now — neither bridle nor blows of the whip,
Not cliffs and cavernous rocks and watercourses that lie
In his path and whirl away mountains their spate undermines.
The famed Sabellian boar now whets his tusks and charges,
Tramples the ground before him, rubs his ribs against trees,
And makes a defensive armour of his shoulders on either flank.
Think of a young man, burning with cruel love to the bone:
Think of him, late in the blindfold night swimming the narrows
That are vexed by headlong gales, while above his head the huge
Gates of heaven thunder and the seas collide with a crash
Against the capes: powerless to recall him his sorrowful parents
And the girl who is soon to die of grief over his body.
Remember the Wine-god's lynxes, the rabid race of wolves
And hounds, and the way unwarlike stags will offer to fight.
But of all, beyond doubt, the fury of mares is the most remarkable:
Venus herself incited
The chariot-team that day they champed the limbs of Glaucus.
In heat, they'll range over Gargarus and across the roaring
Ascanius, they'll climb mountains and swim rivers.
The moment that flame is kindled within their passionate flesh
(In spring above all, when warmth returns to their bones) the whole herd
Wheels to face the west wind high up there on the rocks;
They snuff the light airs and often without being mated
Conceive, for the wind — astounding to tell — impregnates them:

[Lines 245-275]

Over the rocks and cliffs then, and down the deep dales
They gallop scattering, not towards the east and the dayspring
But to the north and north-west
And where the south wind arises glooming the sky with cold rain.
Whereupon a clammy fluid, which herdsmen call
Correctly 'hippomanes,' oozes from out their groin —
Hippomanes, by wicked stepmothers much sought after
And mixed with herbs and malignant cantrips to brew a spell.

But time is on the move still, time that will not return,
While we go cruising around this subject whose lore delights us.
So much for herds. The second part of my work remains —
The business of wool-bearing flocks and shaggy she-goats.
Here's work for you, stalwart farmers, and a hope of winning fame.
I'm well aware it's hard to master this subject in words
And honour a theme so constricted: but over those steep and lonely
Places I'm winged by poetry's
Rapture: how grand to go on that ridge where no man before me
Has made his mark wheeling aside down the gentle slope!
Now, worshipful goddess of sheepfolds, grant me a fuller tone!

To begin with, I prescribe that in their cosy pens
The sheep should feed till leafy summer's soon return;
And that you put down plenty of straw and bundles of bracken
On the hard ground, to guard your flock against the wintry
Frost which is apt to give them scab and the nasty foot-rot.
Passing on, I suggest for the goats a stock of flowering
Arbutus, fresh stream-water,
And stalls sheltered from wind, facing the winter sun,
Turned towards the midday, at the time when cold Aquarius
Is setting and asperges the skirts of the dying year.
Goats require as careful looking-after as sheep
(Nor less will their profit be, although Milesian fleeces

Dyed in Tyrian purples fetch you an excellent price);
For their young are more numerous and their yield of milk is large;
The fuller the milk-pails foam from their exhausted udders,
The richer milk you'll get when you squeeze their teats again.
Besides, men clip the beard,
The grizzled chin and bristly coat of the Libyan he-goat,
For use in camps and to make sailcloth for luckless mariners.
Their pasture is an Arcadian forest or height, where they feed
On prickly brambles and on thorn-bushes that love a hillside.
Unherded they remember to come home, they lead their young,
Hardly lift their heavy udders through the half-door.
So take the more trouble, because their demands on human aid
Are less, to guard them from frosts and snowy winds, and to give them
Freely their keep and fodder
Of boughs, leaving your hayloft open throughout the winter.
But when the west winds call and the exquisite warm season
Ushers them out, both sheep and goats, to glade and pasture,
At the first wink of the Morning Star let us wend away
To the frore fields, while the morning is young, the meadow pearly,
And dew so dear to cattle lies on the tender grass.
Then, when the fourth hour of the sun has created a thirst
And the plantations vibrate with the pizzicato of crickets,
I'll bring the flocks to water by wells and by deep ponds,
I'll bid them drink the water that runs in the troughs of ilex.
But now it's the noonday heat, make for a shady combe
Where some great ancient-hearted oak throws out its huge
Boughs, or the wood is black with
A wealth of holm-oak and broods in its own haunted shadow.
Then give them runnels of water again and let them browse
About sundown, when the cool star of evening assuages
The air, and moonlight falls now with dew to freshen the glades,

[Lines 307-337]

And the kingfisher's heard on the shore and the warbler in woody thickets.
　　Shall I tell you of African shepherds, describe to you in my verse
Their grazing-grounds and the scattered shanties wherein they dwell?
Daylong and nightlong often, yes, for a month on end
Their flocks go grazing into the desert distances
Where no habitation is, so broad stretches the plain.
The African herdsman takes everything with him — his hearth and home,
Weapons, hound and quiver:
Just so will the fierce Roman, armed as his fathers were,
Make a forced march, though carrying excessive weight of equipment,
Till the column is halted, the camp pitched, the foe surprised.
　　Not so among the northern tribes by the Sea of Azof,
And where the Danube swirls muddy with yellow sand
Or beneath the mid-pole Mount Rhodope stretches to east and north.
The cattle are kept in the stalls there;
Not a blade of grass appears on the plain, not a leaf on the trees:
But far as eye can reach earth lies, her features lost
Beneath snowdrifts and ice to a depth of seven fathoms.
It's always winter, always the cold nor-wester blowing.
And worse, the sun can never break through the wan gloom there —
Not when his horses draw him up to the height of heaven,
Not when his chariot brings him to bathe in the blood-red sea.
Films of ice form suddenly over the flowing rivers;
And next, the water is bearing iron wheels on its back
And harbours broad-beamed waggons, that once was a home for ships:
Brass vessels constantly burst, clothes freeze stiff as you wear them,
Wine can be chopped with an axe,
Whole tarns are turned to solid ice, and icicles grow
Bristling on uncombed beards.
All this while the air is one white drift of snow:
Cattle die, the bulky oxen stand about

[Lines 338-368]　　　　54

Shrouded in frost, and herds of deer huddling together
Grow numb beneath new-formed drifts, their antlers barely showing.
Men hunt them not with hounds now, nor do they use the nets,
No scarlet-feathered toils are needed to break their nerve;
But the deer vainly shove at the banked-up snow with their shoulders,
The men attack them at close quarters, they cut them down
Belling loud, and cheerfully shout as they bring them home.
They themselves dig out deep igloos underground
Where they live in carefree leisure, keeping up their fire
With oak from the stack and trunks of elm they trundle to the hearth.
Here they while away the darkness in games, and gladly
Make do with beer and a rough cider for draughts of wine.
Such are the tameless tribes
Of the north, beneath the seven-starred Bear much buffeted
By east winds, wearing the tawny fur of beasts for protection.

    If wool-growing is your business, beware of barbed vegetation,
Goose-grass and star-thistle: avoid too rich a grazing:
Choose from the start a flock both white and soft of fleece.
Reject any ram, however pure a white his wool,
If the tongue beneath his moist palate is black, for he'll breed
Lambs with black-spotted fleeces —
Reject, and look round for another ram on the crowded sheep-run.
With the lure of such snowy wool, if the legend is worth belief,
Pan, god of Arcady, captivated and tricked the Moon,
Calling her down to the deep woods — a call she disdained not.

    But the man who is out for milk should bring plenty of clover,
Trefoil and salted grass to the goat-pens, and do it in person.
Since a thirst for water is whetted thus, and their udders swell,
And they'll impart to the milk a faint sub-flavour of salt.
Many will even keep the new-born kids from their mothers
By fixing iron-spiked muzzles over the suckling mouths.

[Lines 369-399]

The milk they obtain at dawn or
During the day, they cheese at night: the evening milk
They pack off at dawn in frails and the shepherd takes it to town,
Or sprinkle lightly with salt and put it by for the winter.

    Last but not least, the care of your dogs: let them feed together
On fattening whey — swift greyhound pups and alert mastiffs.
You'll never need to fear
Robbers by night in your cattle-pens or a raid of wolves
Or Spanish brigands creeping behind you, while they're on guard.
Often too men hunt the timid wild ass, the hare
And fallow deer with hounds:
Often again their barking will start a wild boar and drive him
From where he wallows in the wood; or in full cry they'll hunt a
Noble stag over the uplands and manœuvre him towards the nets.

    It's wise also to burn sweet juniper in the byres,
Rout out the fetid-smelling snakes with fumes of gum.
When stalls go long uncleaned, you'll commonly find beneath them
A viper lurking, hater of light, unhealthy to touch;
Or the serpent, whose habit is to creep into dark corners of buildings
(A damnable plague to oxen) and inject the herd with his poison,
Lies lodged in earth. Take stones, shepherd, take a stick and strike
Him down as he rears in malice, hissing, his neck puffed out.
He's hidden his cowardly head now
In the hole; his middle folds and the writhing tip of his tail
Unwind, as the last coil slithers away slowly.
Or take that evil watersnake of Calabrian woods
Who bowls around with upright port; his back is scaly,
His belly long and marked all over in big blotches:
That one, while streams are still issuing from their source
And earth remains dank with wet spring and the rainy south wind,
Living in ponds, housekeeping on river-banks, will cram his

Black maw with fish and garrulous frogs immoderately.
But when the swamp dries out and a hot sun splits the earth
He darts onto dry land, rolling his flame-shot eyes,
And raves through the meadows, mad with thirst, crazy with heat.
I only hope I shall never be tempted to sleep in the open
Or repose on a forest ridge
Among the grass, when that one has cast his slough and glides out
Gleaming in youth, leaving his young or his eggs at home,
Erect to the sun, forked tongue flickering between his lips.

      Diseases too will I treat of — their causes, signs and symptoms.
Rotting mange afflicts a flock when chilly rain
And hoar-frost of midwinter work deep into the living
Flesh, or when the sheep have been sheared and clotted sweat
Clings to their unwashed bodies and tangles of briar have cut them.
As a remedy, the whole flock is dipped in running water
By the flock-masters, the ram plunged in a pool to soak
His fleece and float downstream;
Or the shorn bodies are smeared with bitter olive-lees,
And a salve is compounded of silver oxide, native sulphur,
Pitch, emollient wax-paste,
Squills and stinking hellebore and black bitumen:
Though indeed there's no better method of inducing in this disease
A favourable crisis than to cut away with a knife
The putrid place; for the malady lives and thrives by concealment,
As long as the shepherd, unwilling to lay a hand on the wound
And heal it, merely sits back and prays for some improvement.
Further, when pain courses through bone and marrow of the bleating
Flock and a dry fever is wasting their limbs away,
It's well to bleed the artery that throbs in their hoof, and thus
Reduce the rage of the fever:
That's what the Macedonians do and the tough Gelonians,

[Lines 431-461]

Migrating to Rhodope or the wastes by the river Danube —
Men who drink their milk curdled with horses' blood.
If you notice from far one sheep more often seeking the shade's
Comfort, cropping the top of the grass more languidly,
Lagging behind the rest, lying down in the middle of the meadow
Where it grazes, and going off by itself as night descends,
You must nip that evil in the bud, you must use your knife and kill
Before its dread contagion creeps through the oblivious flock.
Thicker and faster than squalls of wind that tear at the sea's face
Come many diseases of cattle,
Killing not one here and there, but a whole summer pasture —
The lambs, the dams, the whole lot of them root and branch.
You'd bear me out, if you went to look at the lofty Alps,
The hill forts of Bavaria, the fields beside Timavo;
It happened long ago here, but you'd see the derelict ranches
Of sheep, old grazings empty up to the far horizon.

  For here it was that once the sky fell sick and a doleful
Season came, all hectic with the close heat of autumn,
And it killed off the whole gamut of cattle and wild beasts.
Infected their drinking pools and put a blight on their fodder.
Death took them by two stages:
When parching thirst had seared the veins and shrivelled the poor limbs,
Watery humours broke out again in flux till the bones all
Rotted and melted piecemeal as the malady ran its course.
Often a victim, brought to the altar for sacrifice,
At the moment they placed the white-ribboned tiara of wool upon it
Fell down dying among them, while the acolytes delayed.
Or, if the priest had killed in time, he could not kindle
To flame the filaments laid on the altar, nor could the seer
Make any sense of them:
The knife beneath the throat was barely stained with blood,

A meagre trickle of bloody matter just tinged the sand.
Now over the rank pasture calves are dying by droves,
Gasping out their life amid the abundant mangers:
Now rabies comes to good-tempered dogs; a painful cough
Racks the sick swine, and their throats swell and they suffocate.
The horse, a prize-winner once, takes no more pride in his paces,
Forgets the grass, turns away from water, keeps on stamping
The ground; sweat comes and goes on his dejected ears —
A cold sweat meaning death:
The hide feels dry if you stroke him, stubborn and harsh to the touch.
Such are the earlier signs he gives of a mortal sickness.
But when the disease begins to reach a deadlier stage,
The eyes are inflamed, the breath comes deep and dragging, broken
By heavy groans, the long flanks heave with profound sobs,
Out of the nostrils oozes
Black blood, the tongue is rough and swells in the throat and blocks it.
Some use it was to insert a drenching-horn and give them
Wine: it seemed the one thing that would restore the dying.
But soon this remedy proved fatal, the sick revived
Only to rave in madness till under the mortal plague
(God send something better to good men, and leave to our foes that error!)
Teeth bared, they savaged their own limbs and tore themselves to shreds.
Watch that bull, steaming from the weight of the iron coulter!
He drops in his tracks, his mouth drools with a bloody foam,
A last groan lifts to heaven. Sadly the ploughman goes
To unyoke the bullock mourning his butty's death: the plough
Stays there, stuck in the middle of the field they never finished.
No tall trees' shade, no gentle
Meads will console the beast, no becks brighter than amber
Scampering down over rocks to the plain: relaxed and flabby
Grow the long flanks, listless and dazed the downcast eye,

Slowly the neck droops dispirited to the ground.
He toiled for us and served us, he turned the difficult earth
With the plough, — and what does it profit him? Yet these were never
Drinkers of wine, nor harmed their health by incessant banquets:
No, their diet is leaves and simple grass alone,
Their cup is the clear springs
And hurrying streams, no cares disquiet their healthy sleep.
    At no other time, or so they tell us, in those parts
Were oxen rarely obtained for Juno's rites, and chariots
Hauled to high votive-shrines by ill-matched buffalo teams.
Painfully men scratched at the soil with mattocks, used their
Own nails to cover in the seed corn, harnessed their necks
To tug the creaking waggons over a towering hillside.
Wolves lurk no longer in ambush around the folds, nor lope
Towards the flock at night: more desperate their affairs
And make them tame. Now timid fallow-deer and elusive
Stags wander amongst the hounds and about men's houses.
Now the deepwater tribes, yes, all the swimming creatures
Lie on the shore's edge, washed by the waves like shipwrecked bodies,
And seals take refuge in rivers they never swam before.
The viper perishes too, in vain defence of her winding
Lair; and the startled snake, his scales standing on end.
The air's precarious even for birds; they plunge down dead,
Leaving their life in the clouds.
Beside all this, changes of diet achieved nothing,
Cures they invented only killed; healers gave up —
Chiron son of Phillyra, Amythaon's son Melampus.
From hell's black country came the pale Tisiphone raging
Into broad daylight, fear and plague galloped on before her,
Higher and hungrier rose her head day after day.
Bleatings and mooings went up, a multitudinous cry,

From streams, parched river-banks and all the prostrate hills.
And now they died by whole companies, and the corpses
Rotting with vile decay lay piled in the very sheep-folds,
Till men had learnt to put them in pits, covered with earth.
The hide was no good, and no man
Could cleanse the carcase in water or burn it up with fire:
You could not even shear the fleece, it was so corroded
With the foul pus, or work that rotten wool in the loom:
But if you were so foolhardy as to wear the hideous garment,
Inflamed pustules and a noxious-smelling sweat appeared
All over your limbs: not long then
Before the fiery curse ate up your tettered frame.

[Lines 555-566

BOOK FOUR

BOOK FOUR

Next I come to the manna, the heavenly gift of honey.
Look kindly on this part too, my friend. I'll tell of a tiny
Republic that makes a show well worth your admiration —
Great-hearted leaders, a whole nation whose work is planned,
Their morals, groups, defences — I'll tell you in due order.
A featherweight theme: but one that can load me with fame, if only
No wicked fairy cross me, and the Song-god come to my call.

For a start you must find your bees a suitable home, a position
Sheltered from wind (for wind will stop them carrying home
Their forage), a close where sheep nor goats come butting in
To jump on the flowers, nor blundering heifer stray to flick
The dew from the meadow and stamp its springing grasses down.
Discourage the lizard, too, with his lapis-lazuli back,
From their rich folds, the bee-eater and other birds,
And the swallow whose breast was blooded once by a killer's hand:
For these wreak wholesale havoc, snap up your bees on the wing
And bear them off as a tit-bit for their ungentle nestlings.
But mind there's a bubbling spring nearby, a pool moss-bordered,
And a rill ghosting through the grass:
See, too, that a palm or tall oleaster shadow the entrance,
For thus, when the new queens lead out the earliest swarms —
The spring all theirs — and the young bees play, from hive unprisoned,
The bank may be handy to welcome them in out of the heat
And the tree meet them halfway and make them at home in its foliage.
Whether the water flows or is stagnant, fling in the middle
Willow boughs criss-cross and big stones,
That the bees may have plenty of bridges to stand on and dry their wings

[Lines 1-27]

At the summer sun, in case a shower has caught them loitering
Or a gust of east wind ducked them suddenly in the water.
Green spurge-laurel should grow round about, wild thyme that perfumes
The air, masses of savory rich-breathing, and violet beds
Sucking the channelled stream.

     Now for the hive itself. Remember, whether you make it
By stitching concave bark or weaving tough withies together,
To give it a narrow doorway: for winter grips and freezes
The honey, and summer's melting heat runs it off to waste.
Either extreme is feared by the bees. It is not for fun
That they're so keen on caulking with wax the draughty chinks
In their roof, and stuff the rim of their hive with flowery pollen,
Storing up for this very job a glue they have gathered
Stickier than bird-lime or pitch from Anatolia.
Often too, if reports are true, they dig deep shelters
Underground and keep house there, or out of the way are found
In a sandstone hollow or the heart of a rotten tree.
None the less, you should smear with smooth mud their chinky chambers
Solicitously for warmth, and lay a thin dressing of leaves.
Don't have a yew too close to their house, or burn in a brazier
Reddening crab-shells: never risk them near a bog,
Or where there's a stink of mud, or a rock formation echoes
Hollow when struck and returns your voice like a ghostly reflection.

     For the rest, when the golden sun has driven winter to ground
And opened up all the leagues of the sky in summer light,
Over the glades and woodlands at once they love to wander
And suck the shining flowers and delicate sip the streams.
Sweet then is their strange delight
As they cherish their children, their nestlings: then with craftsmanship they
Hammer out the fresh wax and mould the tacky honey.
Then, as you watch the swarm bursting from hive and heavenward

Soaring, and floating there on the limpid air of summer —
A vague and wind-warped column of cloud to your wondering eyes: —
Notice them, how they always make for fresh water and leafy
Shelter. Here you shall sprinkle fragrances to their taste —
Crushed balm, honeywort humble —
Make a tinkling noise round about and clash the Mother-god's cymbals.
They will settle down of their own accord in the place you have perfumed,
And crawl to the innermost room for rest, as their custom is.

But now, suppose they have sallied to battle: for between
Two queens there often arises trouble that comes to war.
At once, from afar, forewarned you will be of the mob's anger,
Their hearts spoiling for a fight:
Martial, a brazen harshness, a roar rebuking the laggard
You hear, and a cry that is like the abrupt blasts of a trumpet.
Then, all agog, their wings quivering, they come together,
Stings are sharpened on beaks, sinews braced for action,
And around the queen in their hordes, right up to the queen's headquarters
They demonstrate, they challenge the foe with fearsome shouts.
So, on a dry spring day, when the sky's prairies are open,
They deploy from their gates, they charge together, in heaven's height
There's a din; they meet and scrimmage, forming a monster ball, and
Headlong they tumble down, thicker than hail in the air
Or a shower of acorns raining down from a shaken oak.
Illustrious of wing, through the battle-line the monarchs
Move, vast passions agitating their little breasts,
Obstinate not to give in till superior weight of numbers
Has forced one side or the other to turn their backs in flight.
And all these epic battles and turbulent hearts you can silence
By flinging a handful of dust.

But, when you have recalled both the leaders from combat,
The one that appears worsted you must kill, lest she prove a waste

[Lines 59-89]

And a nuisance, and let the winner be absolute in the kingdom.
The one will be all aglow in golden-painted mail —
Two kinds there are — this one is the better, taking the eye
With her form and the flash of her shining scales; that other is shaggy
From laziness, a low and pot-bellied crawler, a bad lot.
As the two queens differ in aspect, so in physique their subjects.
For some are unkempt and squalid, like a traveller when he comes
Athirst off a dusty road and spits the grit from his dry mouth;
While others gleam and glitter,
Their bodies perfectly marked in a pattern of shining gold.
These are the better breed: from these at the right season
Sweet honey you'll get — not sweet so much as pure, and fit
To soften your wine's harsh flavour.
But when the swarms fly aimlessly and sport in the sky,
Looking down on their combs, leaving the hives to cool,
You must put a stop to this empty and irresponsible play.
It is not hard to stop.
Tear off the wings of their queens: while these wait on the ground,
No bee will dare to leave his base or take off for a flight.
Let gardens breathing a scent of yellow flowers allure them:
Let the god of gardens, who watches for birds and robbers, keep them
Safe with his hook of willow.
The bee-keeper for his part should fetch down thyme and pine
From the hills above, and plant them broadly around the bees' home:
His hands should grow work-hardened, bedding the soil with fertile
Shoots, watering them well.

    Indeed, were it not that already my work has made its landfall
And I shorten sail and eagerly steer for the harbour mouth,
I'd sing perhaps of rich gardens, their planning and cultivation,
The rose beds of Paestum that blossom twice in a year,
The way endive rejoices to drink from a rivulet,

The bank all green with celery, the cucumber snaking
Amid the grass and swelling to greatness: I'd not forget
Late-flowering narcissus or gum-arabic's ringlet shoots,
Pale ivy, shore-loving myrtle.
I remember once beneath the battlements of Oebalia,
Where dark Galaesus waters the golden fields of corn,
I saw an old man, a Corycian, who owned a few poor acres
Of land once derelict, useless for arable,
No good for grazing, unfit for the cultivation of vines.
But he laid out a kitchen garden in rows amid the brushwood,
Bordering it with white lilies, verbena, small-seeded poppy.
He was happy there as a king. He could go indoors at night
To a table heaped with dainties he never had to buy.
His the first rose of spring, the earliest apples in autumn:
And when grim winter still was splitting the rocks with cold
And holding the watercourses with curb of ice, already
That man would be cutting his soft-haired hyacinths, complaining
Of summer's backwardness and the west winds slow to come.
His bees were the first to breed,
Enriching him with huge swarms: he squeezed the frothy honey
Before anyone else from the combs: he had limes and a wealth of pine trees:
And all the early blossom, that clothed his trees with promise
Of an apple crop, by autumn had come to maturity.
He had a gift, too, for transplanting in rows the far-grown elm,
The hardwood pear, the blackthorn bearing its weight of sloes,
And the plane that already offered a pleasant shade for drinking.
But these are matters the strict scope of my theme forbids me:
I must pass them by, and leave them for later men to enlarge on.
    Well then, let me speak of the natural gifts that God himself
Bestowed on the bees, their reward
For obeying the charms — the chorus and clashing brass of the priests —

[Lines 121-151]

And feeding the king of heaven when he hid in that Cretan cave,
They alone have their children in common, a city united
Beneath one roof and a life under established laws:
They know a native country, are sure of hearth and home.
Aware that winter is coming, they use the summer days
For work, and put their winnings into a common pool.
Some are employed in getting food, and by fixed agreement
Work on the fields: some stay within their fenced abode,
With tear of daffodil and gummy resin of tree-bark
Laying the first foundation of the honeycomb, then hanging
The stickfast wax: others bring up the young bees, the hope
Of their people: others press
The pure honey and cram the cells with that crystal nectar.
Some, allotted the duty of sentry-go at the gates,
Keep an eye out for showers and a sign of clouds in heaven,
Relieve incoming bees of their burden, or closing ranks
Shoo the drones — that work-shy gang — away from the bee-folds.
The work goes on like wildfire, the honey smells of thyme.
Thus when the Blacksmith Giants work double shifts to forge
Thunderbolts out of the stubborn ore, some ply the bellows
Of bull-skin, and others plunge the hissing metal in troughs:
And while Mount Aetna moans beneath their anvils' stress
They raise their arms with the powerful alternate rhythm of cranks,
They keep the iron turning in the close grip of their tongs.
So, to compare small things
With great, an inborn love of possession impels the bees
Each to his own office. The old are the town's wardens,
Who wall the honeycombs and frame the intricate houses.
Tired, as the night deepens, the young return from labour,
Their legs laden with thyme: they feed afar on the arbute,
The silvery willow, the spurge laurel, the fire-blush saffron,

[Lines 152-182]   70

The lime blossom so rich, the rust-red martagon lily.
For one and all one work-time, and a like rest from work.
At morning they hurry from the hives, all helter-skelter: again,
When the Evening Star has told them to leave their meadow pasture,
They make for home, they refresh themselves. What a murmuring
You hear as they drone around their policies and doorsteps!
Later, they settle down in their cells for the night, a silence
Falls, a drowsy fatigue falls.
If rain threatens, be sure they'll not roam too far afield
From their hives: they mistrust the sky, should an east wind be due:
At such times safely beneath the walls of their town they forage
Around, making brief excursions, and often carry some ballast,
As dinghies do to stiffen them in a high sea — they lift
Wee stones, and with these they weather the cloud-tossed solitudes.

    Most you shall marvel at this habit peculiar to bees —
That they have no sexual union: their bodies never dissolve
Lax into love, nor bear with pangs of birth their young.
But all by themselves from leaves and sweet herbs they will gather
Their children in their mouths, keep up the queenly succession
And the birth-rate, restore the halls and the realm of wax.
Often, too, as they wander they bruise their wings on hard
Rocks, happy to die in harness beneath their burdens —
Such is their love for flowers, their pride in producing honey.
Though short their course of life, and death may catch them early,
(Seven summers they have at most),
The race remains immortal, for many years survive
The family fortunes, their fathers are known to the fourth generation.
Besides, they esteem royalty more than Egypt does or enormous
Lydia even, or the peoples of Parthia, or the Mede by Hydaspes.
Let the queen be safe — they are bound by a single faith and purpose:
Lose her — then unity's gone, and they loot the honey cells

[Lines 183-213]

They built themselves, and break down the honeycomb's withy wall.
Guardian of all their works she is. They hold her in awe.
Thick is their humming murmur as they crowd around her and mob her.
Often they chair her shoulder high: and in war they shelter
Her body with theirs, desiring the wounds of a noble death.

    Influenced by these signs and images, some have said
That bees partake of an Essence Divine and drink Heaven's well-springs.
For God (they hold) pervades
All lands, the widespread seas, the abysms of unplumbed sky:
From Whom flocks, herds, men, every wild creature in its kind
Derive at birth the slight, precarious breath of life:
To Him, therefore, all things return at last and in Him
Are re-absorbed — no room for death — and they soar to join
The stars' immortal muster, and reach the heights of heaven.

    If ever you wish to unseal the treasure-vaults of their palace
Where the honey's hoarded, first sprinkle yourself with water,
Rinse your mouth, and release a smoke to chivvy them out.
Twice a year men gather their harvest and heavy produce: —
As soon as Taÿgete the Pleiad has turned her handsome
Face to the earth and spurned with her foot the repulsed ocean;
Or again when, fleeing the star of the rainy Fish, she goes
Gloomily down the sky and is drowned in a winter sea.
Unbounded then is the rage of the bees, provoked they breathe
Venom into their stabs, they cling to your veins and bury
Their stings — oh yes, they put their whole souls into the wound.
But if you fear a hard winter for them and wish to provide for
The future, pitying their bruised spirits and bankrupt estate,
Even then you should trouble to fumigate with thyme
And cut back the empty cells. For often the newt unnoticed
Nibbles the combs, their cubicles are black with light-shunning beetles,
And the drone gate-crashes their dinner:

There's the assassin hornet who, heavier armed than they,
Mixes it: there's the sinister tribe of moths: and Minerva's
Bugbear, the spider, draping his slack nets over the doorway.
But the more exhausted the bees, the keener they'll be to mend
The wreck of their ruined state,
Re-stock the store-rooms and fashion the flowery granaries.

      Since life brings to the bees the same bad luck as to humans,
They may suffer severe illness —
An epidemic you'll know by certain definite signs.
The sick change colour at once, and their faces are deformed
By dreadful emaciation: the bodies of the dead
They carry out of doors and bear in a sad cortège:
With clutching feet they hang
From the doorway, or moon about within their closed mansion
Listless with hunger all, numbed by a cramping cold.
Then there is heard a deeper sound, a hum sustained
As when a chill south wind murmurs among woods
Or the waves of a troubled sea moan and hiss at the ebb-tide
Or fierce flames roar heaving behind a furnace door.
I recommend here that you burn the pungent galbanum,
And instil honey through pipes of reed, going out of your way
To coax the invalid creatures back to familiar food.
It's a good thing also to add the juice of pounded oak-apples,
And dried rose-leaves, or wine boiled rich over a strong fire,
Raisins from the Psythian vine,
Thyme of Attica, and centaury strong-smelling.
There's a flower of the meadow, too, that our farmers call 'amellus':
It's easy enough to find,
For it raises up from a single stool a forest of stems;
Golden the disk, raying out into petals whose dark violet
Is shot with a purple shine:

[Lines 245-275]

Often the gods' altars are adorned with garlands of it:
Its taste is rough to the tongue: shepherds gather it on the close-cropped
Valley slopes and beside the meandering stream of Mella.
Boil the roots of this flower in fragrant wine, and serve it
In basketfuls at their door, a tonic food for the bees.

But if a man's swarm shall suddenly fail him, so that he has no
Source for another brood,
It is time to detail the famous invention of an Arcadian
Bee-master, the process by which he often made
A culture of bees from the putrid blood of slaughtered bullocks.
I'll give you a full account, exploring the earliest sources.
Where the people of Macedonian Canopus, a lucky race,
Live by the wide and standing flood-waters of Nile, and go
The round of their own farmlands in little painted boats;
And where the boundaries of Persia, land of archers, approach,
And the river rolling down
Right from the dark Abyssinians makes a delta of seven mouths
And fertilizers green Egypt's fields with its black sludge —
All this region relies on the artifice I tell of.
First a small place is chosen, a site that is narrowed further
For this same purpose: they close it in with a pantile roof
And prisoning walls: they add
Four windows with slanting lights that face towards the four winds.
A two-year-old calf is obtained, whose horns are beginning to curve
From his forehead. They stopper up, though he struggle wildly, his two
Nostrils and breathing mouth, and they beat him to death with blows
That pound his flesh to pulp but leave the hide intact.
Battened down in that narrow room they leave him, under his ribs
Laying fresh cassia and thyme and broken branches.
This is done as soon as a west wind ruffles the water,
Before the meadows are flushed with vernal colour, before

The talkative martin hangs her nest under the rafters.
Meanwhile, within the marrowy bones of the calf, the humours
Grow warm, ferment, till appear creatures miraculous —
Limbless at first, but soon they fidget, their wings vibrate,
And more, more they sip, they drink the delicate air:
At last they come pouring out, like a shower from summer clouds,
Or thick and fast as arrows
When Parthian archers, their bowstrings throbbing, advance to battle.

     What god was it, my Muse, that worked this miracle for us?
Who caused this novel practice to cross the minds of men?
A shepherd called Aristaeus was leaving Thessalian Tempe,
His bees — so the story goes — destroyed by disease and famine;
And glum he stood by the hallowed river-head, invoking,
Upbraiding the one who bore him.
'O mother, my mother Cyrene, who dwell in the deep below
This pool, why did you bear me from the glorious seed of godhead
(If indeed, as you tell me, the god Apollo of Troas begat me)
To be fate's target? Where, where has your love for me flown?
Why tell me to hope for heaven?
Look, even this mere grace of mortal life, which I won
So hardly by craft and much resourcefulness from the care of
Harvest and herd — though you are my mother — I must abandon.
Go on, then, with your own hand grub up my happy orchards,
Be my enemy, set fire to my sheep-folds, murder the harvests,
Blast the sown fields, hack down the vines with a brutal axe,
If you find my praise so irksome.'
     His mother heard that cry from her room beneath the river.
The nymphs, her companions, were carding
Fleeces of Miletus dyed a rich glass-green colour —
Drymo, Xantho, Ligea, Phyllodoce were their names
And their tresses were loose and glittering about their snowshine necks:

[Lines 307-337]

Cydippe too and corn-blonde Lycorias, one a virgin,
The other but now had felt her travail pains for the first time:
Clio and Beroe her sister, both Ocean princesses,
Both of them gold-adorned and girt with dappled skins:
The Ephyrean was there, and Opis, and Deiopeia,
And Arethusa the fleetfoot, her arrows at last laid by.
Clymene was telling the story of Vulcan, the trouble he took
In vain, and how Mars tricked him and stole his sweet away,
Recounting the gods' continual amours from Chaos onwards.
While the nymphs were charmed by her song and the soft wool curled
Once more his mother's ears   [from their distaffs,
Thrilled to the shepherd's grief, and all of them on their glassy
Thrones were astounded: then, before the rest, Arethusa
Glanced forth, raising her golden head out of the pool,
And called from afar. 'You are right to be fluttered by such a wild
Lament, sister Cyrene, for he — your fondest care —
Aristaeus is weeping at the waterside of his father,
Naming you, calling you cruel.'
Then, heart frantic with fresh alarm, his mother said,
'Bring, oh bring him to me! No harm for him to approach
The gods' threshold.' At once she bade the stream roll back
And leave a wide path, an entrance for him. But the water
Stood up on end in a mountainous curve, stood all around him,
Laid him in its huge lap and bore him beneath the surface.
Marvelling now at his mother's home and aqueous kingdom —
The pools enclosed in caverns, the sighing woods of weed —
He went along: the enormous passage of waters dazed him,
For he viewed all the rivers that glide below great earth
Far and wide — Phasis, Lycus,
The spring from which the deep Enipeus first leaps forth,
The source of father Tiber and the flowing Anio,

Of Hypanis roaring down through rocks, Mysian Caicus,
Of Eridanus, depicted with gilded horns on his bull-head —
Eridanus, than which through fertile lands no river
Rushes with more momentum to the pansy-purple sea.
So he reached the overhanging roof of his mother's bower
Fashioned in porous stone, and she heard his fond lament.
Her sisters washed his hands
Duly with pure water and fetched the nappy towels:
Others loaded the table with a banquet and laid the brimming
Goblets, and fed the altar fire with Arabian incense.
Then his mother cried, 'Take up your cups of wine! Let us drink
A toast to Ocean!' Herself to Ocean at once she prayed,
Father of the universe, and the sisterhood of nymphs
Who are wardens over a hundred woods, a hundred rivers.
Three times did she pour on the hallowed hearth-fire the pure nectar,
Three times did the lowly flame leap up to ceiling height —
A sign that gave him heart.

    'There dwells in the Mediterranean a seer,' she began to say —
'Sea-blue Proteus, one who drives through the mighty deep
His chariot drawn by harnessed fish and two-legged horses.
He is visiting now the Macedonian ports and Pallene
His birth-place. Him we nymphs and ancient Nereus hold
In honour, for he knows all
That is, that has been, and all that is about to be —
Knows all by the god Neptune's grace, whose herds of monsters
And hideous seals he pastures in meadows submarine.
This seer, my son, you must bind in fetters before he'll tell you
The whole truth of your bees' sickness and put things right.
Except to violence he yields not one word of advice; entreaties
Have no effect: you must seize him, offer him force and fetters,
On which in the end his wiles will dash themselves to waste.

　　　　　　　　[Lines 369-399]

I myself, when the sun has flamed to full meridian,
When grass is thirsty and shade more grateful to the flocks,
Will lead you up to that ancient's den, where he withdraws
Tired from the waves, that easily you may attack him sleeping.
But when you have him fast in a handhold and fettered, then
With the guise and visage of various wild beasts he'll keep you guessing:
Suddenly he'll turn into a bristling boar, a black tiger,
A laminated dragon or lioness tawny-necked,
Or go up in a shrill burst of flame and thus from his fetters
Escape, or give you the slip gliding off in a trickle of water.
But the more he transforms himself,
The tighter, my son, you must strain the shackles that bind his body,
Until at last it changes back to the first likeness
You saw at the start when his eyes were closing down in sleep.'
     Thus she spoke, and she sprayed a perfume of pure ambrosia
Over her son's body,
So that his comely curls wafted a pleasing fragrance
And his limbs grew strong and lithe . . . There is a giant cave
Hallowed out from the flank of a mountain where myriad waves
Forced by the wind drive in and among its coves are dispersed —
A cosy anchorage once for sailors caught in a storm.
Proteus shelters within behind a huge rock-barrier.
Here the nymph puts her son in a hiding-place out of the light,
Standing herself at a distance, dim in the drapes of mist.
Now the raving Dog Star that burns parched Indians
Glared in the sky, and the fiery sun had finished half
His course: the grass was scorched: the river-beds, dry and gasping,
Roasted in the sun's rays, were baked to a hot mud.
Now Proteus came to his customed
Den from the water: around him the dripping tribes of the deep
Frolicked, flinging the bitter spray far and wide about them.

All over the beach the seals were sprawled for their siesta.
The wizard himself, just like a herdsman might on the mountains,
What evening herds the calves homeward out of their pasture
And wolves prick up their ears hearing the lambs bleating,
Sat in the midst of them on a rock and took their tally.
Aristaeus saw his chance:
Scarcely letting the old man lay down his weary limbs,
He rushed him with a great shout and shackled him where he lay.
The wizard for his part remembered well his magic
And turned himself into all kinds of uncanny things —
Became a fire, a fearful wild beast, a flowing river.
But, seeing that no deception could spirit him away, beaten
He returned to himself and spoke at last in human tones.
'Boldest of youths, who bade you
Approach my house? What do you want with me?' The other,
'You know, Proteus, you know very well: for nothing escapes you.
Stop being stubborn. Obeying the gods' commands we are come
To ask the oracle how to revive my drooping fortunes.'
So much he said. At last now the seer convulsively
Rolled his glaring eyes so they shone with a glassy light,
Harshly ground his teeth, and thus gave tongue to Fate.—
      'Not without sanction divine is the anger that hunts you down.
Great is the crime you pay for. Piteous Orpheus calls
This punishment on you. Well you deserve it. If destiny
So wills it. Bitter his anguish for the wife was taken from him.
Headlong beside that river she fled you. She never saw,
Poor girl, her death there, deep in the grass before her feet —
The watcher on the river-bank, the savage watersnake.
The band of wood-nymphs, her companions, filled with their crying
The hilltops: wailed the peaks of Rhodope: high Pangaea,
The unwarlike land of Rhesus,

[Lines 431-461]

The Getae lamented, and Hebrus, and Attic Orithyia.
Orpheus, sick to the heart, sought comfort of his hollow lyre:
You, sweet wife, he sang alone on the lonely shore,
You at the dawn of day he sang, at day's decline you.
The gorge of Taenarus even, deep gate of the Underworld,
He entered, and that grove where fear hangs like a black fog:
Approached the ghostly people, approached the King of Terrors
And the hearts that know not how to be touched by human prayer.
But, by his song aroused from Hell's nethermost basements,
Flocked out the flimsy shades, the phantoms lost to light,
In number like to the millions of birds that hide in the leaves
When evening or winter rain from the hills has driven them —
Mothers and men, the dead
Bodies of great-heart heroes, boys and unmarried maidens,
Young men laid on the pyre before their parents' eyes —
And about them lay the black ooze, the crooked reeds of Cocytus,
Bleak the marsh that barred them in with its stagnant water,
And the Styx coiling nine times around corralled them there.
Why, Death's very home and holy of holies was shaken
To hear that song, and the Furies with steel-blue snakes entwined
In their tresses; the watch-dog Cerberus gaped open his triple mouth;
Ixion's wheel stopped dead from whirling in the wind.
And now he's avoided every pitfall of the homeward path,
And Eurydice, regained, is nearing the upper air
Close behind him (for this condition has Proserpine made),
When a moment's madness catches her lover off his guard —
Pardonable, you'd say, but Death can never pardon.
He halts. Eurydice, his own, is now on the lip of
Daylight. Alas! he forgot. His purpose broke. He looked back.
His labour was lost, the pact he had made with the merciless king
Annulled. Three times did thunder peal over the pools of Avernus.

[Lines 462-492]   80

"Who," she cried, "has doomed me to misery, who has doomed us?
What madness beyond measure? Once more a cruel fate
Drags me away, and my swimming eyes are drowned in darkness.
Good-bye. I am borne away. A limitless night is about me
And over the strengthless hands I stretch to you, yours no longer."
Thus she spoke: and at once from his sight, like a wisp of smoke,
Thinned into air, was gone.
Wildly he grasped at shadows, wanting to say much more,
But she did not see him; nor would the ferryman of the Inferno
Let him again cross the fen that lay between them.

What could he do, where go, his wife twice taken from him?
What lament would move Death now? What deities hear his song?
Cold she was voyaging now over the Stygian stream.
Month after month, they say, for seven months alone
He wept beneath a crag high up by the lonely waters
Of Strymon, and under the ice-cold stars poured out his dirge
That charmed the tigers and made the oak trees follow him.
As a nightingale he sang that sorrowing under a poplar's
Shade laments the young she has lost, whom a heartless ploughman
Has noticed and dragged from the nest unfledged; and the nightingale
Weeps all night, on a branch repeating the piteous song,
Loading the acres around with the burden of her lament.
No love, no marriage could turn his mind away from grief:
Alone through Artic ice, through the snows of Tanais, over
Frost-bound Riphaean plateaux
He ranged, bewailing his lost Eurydice and the wasted
Bounty of Death. In the end Thracian Bacchantes, flouted
By his neglect, one night in the midst of their Master's revels
Tore him limb from limb and scattered him over the land.
But even then that head, plucked from the marble-pale
Neck, and rolling down mid-stream on the river Hebrus —

81 [Lines 493-523]

That voice, that cold, cold tongue cried out "Eurydice!"
Cried "Poor Eurydice!" as the soul of the singer fled,
And the banks of the river echoed, echoed "Eurydice!" '
     Thus Proteus spake, and dived into the sea's depths,
And where he dived the water, foaming, spun in a funnel.
     Cyrene waited and spoke a word to her frightened son:
'You may cast your cares away,'
She said, 'for here is the whole truth of your bees' sickness
And the death they were dealt by the nymphs with whom Eurydice
Danced in the deep woods. So offer them gifts and make your
Peace with them, and pray to the Gracious Ones of the grove.
They will answer your prayers with forgiveness, they will forget their anger.
But first let me tell you the form your orisons must take.
Choose four bulls of excellent body that now on the heights of
Green Lycaeus are grazing,
And as many heifers whose necks have never felt the yoke.
Build for these four altars beside the lofty shrines
Of the goddesses, and let the sacred blood from their throats,
Then leave the oxen's bodies alone in a leafy thicket.
When the ninth day has dawned
You shall send oblivion's poppies as a funeral gift to Orpheus,
Slay a calf in honour of Eurydice placated,
Slaughter a black ewe and go to the thicket again.'
     Without delay he acts at once on his mother's advice:
He comes to the shrine, erects — as she told him — altars, and brings
Four bulls of excellent body
With as many heifers whose necks have never felt the yoke:
When the ninth day has dawned,
Sends funeral gifts to Orpheus and goes to the thicket again.
Here, to be sure, a miracle sudden and strange to tell of
They behold: from the oxen's bellies all over their rotting flesh

Creatures are humming, swarming through the wreckage of their ribs —
Huge and trailing clouds of bees, that now in the treetops
Unite and hang like a bunch of grapes from the pliant branches.
    Thus of agriculture and the care of flocks I sang
And forestry, while great Caesar fired his lightnings and conquered
By deep Euphrates, and gave justice to docile peoples,
Winning his way to the Immortals.
This was the time when I, Virgil, nurtured in sweetest
Parthenope, did follow unknown to fame the pursuits
Of peace, who dallied with pastoral verse, and by youth emboldened,
Tityrus, sang of you in the shade of a spreading beech.